WHAT ANIMAL ARE YOU?

David Is a Dolphin, Molly Is a Moose...
Determine what animal you're most
like based on your personal behaviors,
predilections, and tendencies!

By Jeremy Bronson
Illustrated by Liz Phang

S0-AAZ-732

rabbit's
foot
press™

A division of SPS Studios, Inc.
Boulder, Colorado.

Library of Congress Catalog Card Number: 2002006112

ISBN: 1-58786-010-4

Manufactured in the United States of America.

First Printing: June 2002

♻ Printed on recycled paper.

This book is printed on fine quality, laid embossed, 80 lb. paper. This paper has been specially produced to be acid free (neutral pH) and contains no groundwood or unbleached pulp. It conforms with all the requirements of the American National Standards Institute, Inc., so as to ensure that this book will last and be enjoyed by future generations.

Library of Congress Cataloging-in-Publication Data

Bronson, Jeremy.
  What animal are you?: David is a dolphin, Molly is a moose — / by Jeremy Bronson; illustrated by Liz Phang.
      p. cm.
  "Determine what animal you're most like based on your personal behaviors, predilections, and tendencies!"
    ISBN 1-58786-010-4 (pbk.: alk. paper)
  1. Typology (Psychology) 2. Animals — Psychological aspects. I. Title.
    BF698.3 B76 2002
    155.2'6 — dc21

2002006112
CIP

© 2002 by **SPS Studios, Inc.**
P.O. Box 4549, Boulder, Colorado, 80306.

CONTENTS

INTRODUCTION

Congratulations, reader! If you own the book in your hands right now, you're about to embark on a life-changing adventure through the human mind and across the animal kingdom.

This book combines three wonderful facets of life on earth: 1) the complexity of man's psyche and behavior, 2) the broad array of wild and domesticated animals we see across the globe, and 3) you and your vibrant personality! Allow us to explain:

***What Animal Are You?* allows YOU to determine what animal you're most like based on your personal behaviors, predilections, and tendencies.**

Here's how the book works:

If you turn to page eleven, you'll see a 25-question personality test followed by scoring instructions. Answer each of the multiple-choice questions according to your own personality. Take some time to think about your answers — after all, you don't want to end up a sea otter when you're obviously a beaver. After you answer all the questions, you'll be able to classify yourself into one of six personality groups. Not knowing anything about you yet, we have no idea which group you'll end up in, but we're still willing to bet that you have a terrific smile!

After you're placed into one of the six personality groups, you'll be directed to a specific chapter of the book, where you'll take one more short test. Once you finish, you'll know exactly which animal represents you best. You'll be able to read all about the personality traits associated with that animal. If you read through the descriptions of the other animals in the book, you'll start to see all sorts of similarities to your friends and family. At the very end of the book, we provide a list of celebrities and *their* animal counterparts. You should check it out.

So congratulations, Mr./Ms./Dr. Reader! You're now ready to start taking the test. Have fun!

WARNING!

We should mention that while our book can be fascinating and entertaining, we're certainly not here to give out free hugs and kisses. Not a chance. We're not letting you think you're a mountain lion if you're a parasitic lamprey. **While giving this book to others can build fun and friendship, the potential harsh reality of finding out that you're a cow can destroy relationships.** We thought you should be forewarned.

Well, congratulations, comrade! Now you're *really* prepared to embark on a quest through the pages of this unique treasure of a book. But if you're STILL unsure or you have some more questions, hopefully we can answer them in the next couple of pages.

A BRIEF Q & A SESSION ESPECIALLY FOR YOU

Q. So this book does *what*?

A. Okay. In sum, you take a personality test, and based upon your answers, we help you figure out which animal your personality most resembles. Take the test, tally your score, etc. You'll see what we're talking about.

Q. Will the test really provide an accurate reflection of my personality?

A. Our personality test is based upon scientific Enneagram tests. We believe that our questions, when answered honestly, will do a good job of determining who you really are. If you feel that the test did not accurately classify you, take it again and be extra truthful!

Q. Where does all this animal analysis come from?

A. It all comes from hours of painstaking research, interviews with professionals, and careful observation. Did you know that a rhinoceros sleeps standing up? We did.

Q. Fine. But why should I even care what animal you think I am like?

A. If you're asking this question, you're part of the cynical, non-voting youth of the Apathetic Age. Nevertheless, there are reasons aplenty. Consider:

- When someone says you are just like a dolphin, you can confidently reply that you are in fact just like a shrew.

- Suppose an accountant walks up to you on the street. He says your personality is that of a golden plover. Before, you would have agreed. Now you know that you're actually a shrew.

- Some kid in the locker room says you are a hen. You know to say, "I am not a hen. I am a shrew."

These three reasons should suffice.

Q. Can I thank you for creating this book for me?

A. You betcha! And you're quite welcome!

CONGRATULATIONS TO YOU! You've sure been getting a lot of praise today. Now you're finally ultra-super ready to get going! In just a short while, you'll share a new and exciting bond with the animal kingdom. Good luck, and see you at the finish line!

HOW TO USE THIS BOOK

Step A:

Fill out the personality test with complete honesty.

It's crucial to answer the questions with candor and introspection. You'll be more satisfied with your animal match in the end.

Step B:

Tally your score and determine your animal category.

Go to the chapter corresponding to that category.

Step C:

Fill out the second personality test at the beginning of your chapter.

Then you'll know exactly which animal represents you best. Read through all the other animals in the book, and you'll find all sorts of similarities to the people you know. Finally, pass the book on to a friend, so he or she can enjoy it, too!

AND NOW FOR THE BIG TEST...

Now you're finally ready to put your pencil to the paper. Take a deep breath — you'll do *great*. Just answer honestly, and please take your precious time. Here we go:

1. You know, nothing beats...

- ● a. reading a good book.
- ○ b. playing team sports.
- ○ c. smelling fresh air.
- ○ d. having a friend by your side.
- ○ e. hearing a good secret.
- ○ f. finishing work early so you can enjoy the day.

2. When I go to an IMAX movie theater...

- ○ a. I am stimulated by the mysteries of arctic caves.
- ○ b. my inevitable boredom swiftly shifts into rage.
- ○ c. I just look at the images because I find the narrative confusing.
- ○ d. I always make sure to take a friend with me.
- ○ e. I put a sweater on the seat next to me to avoid proximity to strangers.
- ○ f. the pictures of Mt. Everest remind me of all the work I need to get done.

3. When I look under a microscope...

- ○ a. I marvel at the intricacies of cellular life.
- ○ b. I am reminded of the cells that comprise the sturdy, healthy human body.
- ○ c. I marvel at how small everything is.
- ○ d. I like to have someone near me to set up the slide, focus, etc.
- ○ e. I might say that I saw a euglena even if I'm not sure.
- ○ f. I might write down everything that I noticed about a given sample.

4. Which of the following movies do you like best?

- ○ a. Maybe *2001: A Space Odyssey*.
- ○ b. I'm gonna say *Goodfellas*.
- ○ c. How about *There's Something About Mary*.
- ○ d. I say *Kramer vs. Kramer*.
- ○ e. Definitely *War Games*.
- ○ f. I guess *Cast Away*.

5. When I play recreational sports, I'd say I am best at...

○ a. anticipating my opponent's moves.
○ b. scaring my opponent.
○ c. making friends with my opponent.
○ d. finding a way to "double team" my opponent.
○ e. strategizing against my opponent.
○ f. out-hustling my opponent.

6. I would like to take a delightful vacation to...

○ a. London.
○ b. Spain.
○ c. Trobania.
○ d. Mexico.
○ e. Amsterdam.
○ f. Japan.

7. When I am stuck in traffic...

○ a. I listen to AM radio.
○ b. I curse at the other cars.
○ c. I like to think about my cats.
○ d. I call someone on my cell phone.
○ e. I might follow behind an ambulance that manages to pass through.
○ f. I think about all of the things I could be doing elsewhere.

8. Which of the following Presidents of the United States do you most admire?

○ a. Harry Truman
○ b. Richard Nixon
○ c. George W. Bush
○ d. Ronald Reagan
○ e. Bill Clinton
○ f. Jimmy Carter

9. I enjoy toying with brain teasers and magic tricks because...

○ a. they're fun and challenging.
○ b. they make me feel smart.
○ c. I can tell them to others later.
○ d. they give me a chance to work with others on a problem.
○ e. they allow me to establish my mental superiority.
○ f. if I sit with them long enough, I can usually figure out the answers.

10. Which of the following amazing pets would you most like to own?

○ a. Parrot
○ b. Dog
○ c. Hamster

○ d. Cat
○ e. Snake
○ f. Goldfish

11. I find personal computing to be...

○ a. a good means of obtaining information.
○ b. a way for me to know what others are doing.
○ c. a mess of wires and beeps.
○ d. virtually essential to maintaining myself.
○ e. creepy because of viruses and cyber-stalking.
○ f. useful in getting all my work done.

12. Which of the following celebrities do you most admire?

○ a. Neil Armstrong
○ b. Mike Tyson
○ c. Sarah Michelle Gellar

○ d. Woody Allen
○ e. Steve Jobs
○ f. Bill Bradley

13. When I go to a concert, I like to...

○ a. analyze the music and apply it to my own life later.
○ b. slam dance in the mosh pit.
○ c. look at the T-shirts that are on sale.
○ d. go with a big group of friends.
○ e. buy tickets from scalpers so I don't have to plan that far in advance.
○ f. arrive a little early and leave a little early.

14. I think fist-fighting...

○ a. is not as effective as discussion and resolution.
○ b. is an acceptable means of gaining respect in some situations.
○ c. is bad but sometimes good.
○ d. makes me nervous, and I would want someone else to defend me.
○ e. is not as effective as careful plotting against the enemy.
○ f. is irresponsible and dangerous.

15. Between you and me, the best thing about love is...

○ a. going places together.
○ b. having someone to calm you down.
○ c. Valentine's Day.
○ d. never being alone.
○ e. having someone's complete trust.
○ f. accomplishing goals as one unit.

16. Which of the following activities do you think you would enjoy most?

○ a. Bird watching
○ b. Hunting
○ c. Petting a cat

○ d. Horseback riding
○ e. Trapping small animals
○ f. Going to the zoo

17. You come across a treasure chest on a sidewalk. It has no lock and appears to have no owner. What in the world is your first reaction?

○ a. I would fantasize about its contents and begin to open it up.
○ b. I would push anyone aside who tried to grab the chest first.
○ c. I would bury the treasure chest and dig it up so that I could say I found the buried treasure.
○ d. I would call someone to ask for advice.
○ e. I would disguise myself as a pirate and claim to be the rightful owner of the chest.
○ f. I would probably walk away to avoid potential conflict.

18. If someone punched me in the face while I was eating ice cream in the park, I would immediately...

○ a. feel shocked and then argue with the perpetrator.
○ b. punch the perpetrator in *his* face while *he* was eating ice cream!
○ c. know that fists don't feel nice on faces.
○ d. run frantically to a police officer or nearby acquaintance.
○ e. try to gather witnesses to help my case.
○ f. hold back my temper and calmly move to safety.

19. We know that you love trucks. But which one is your favorite?

○ a. Monster ○ d. Fire
○ b. Bulldozer ○ e. Pickup
○ c. UPS ○ f. Cement mixer

20. If you won the New York Lottery ($40 million jackpot!) with the numbers 12-3-45-2-67-4-23, what would you do with the money?

○ a. I would buy things that enabled me to develop new hobbies or pastimes.

○ b. I would buy something flashy — perhaps a sports car or a mansion.

○ c. I would buy 25 million ice-cream cones and no one could say "no" because I would have all the money in my pocket.

○ d. I would probably worry about losing the money and seek professional assistance.

○ e. I would keep all the money and to figure out how to avoid the immense gift tax.

○ f. I would invest all the money conservatively and enjoy the financial security for myself and future generations of my family.

21. Assuming you drive a 1998 Subaru Outback, which car feature do you most appreciate?

○ a. CD player ○ d. Dual-side airbags
○ b. Four-wheel drive ○ e. Radar police detector
○ c. Round tires ○ f. Power-steering/anti-lock brakes

22. Which of the following is most important for every child to know?

○ a. Our imagination is like baby powder: You may not need it to live, but it feels really good when you put it on.

○ b. You have to be willing to defend yourself if trouble comes your way.

○ c. Stuffed animals are fun to cuddle with but sometimes you should put them in the washing machine.

○ d. You should try to cultivate a group of friends to spend time with.

○ e. More than anything, you should always act according to your best interests.

○ f. Never let yourself become lazy.

23. Now we've all been wondering... which color really is most pleasing to you?

○ a. Green   ○ d. Yellow
○ b. Red   ○ e. Blue
○ c. Orange   ○ f. Purple

24. Which of the following results of the space program do you appreciate most?

○ a. It allows us to discover new scientific truths.
○ b. It allows our country to establish superiority among other political superpowers.
○ c. It will someday allow us to put a man on the moon.
○ d. It gives me something to talk about in conversations.
○ e. It allows us to further utilize satellites so that we can monitor different countries.
○ f. I have never been particularly interested in the space program.

25. As you took this test, which of the following best describes your attitude?

○ a. I guess I enjoyed it. I'm sort of curious to see where we're going with all of this.
○ b. You're wasting my time, and I'm on the verge of burning this book.
○ c. I like to rub soft things against my cheek.
○ d. Pretty interesting, but I think it would work better if someone else filled it out for you.
○ e. I know exactly what animal I'm like already, so let's get going here.
○ f. I took time with each question, so I'm hoping for an accurate evaluation.

END TEST

SCORING

Count how many of each letter you chose in the 25-question test. Then select the letter with the highest total and continue...

TALLY:

_____ If you chose **A** the most, go to Chapter 5 **Page 79**.

_____ If you chose **B** the most, go to Chapter 1 **Page 19**.

_____ If you chose **C** the most, go to Chapter 6 **Page 95**.

_____ If you chose **D** the most, go to Chapter 4 **Page 63**.

_____ If you chose **E** the most, go to Chapter 3 **Page 49**.

_____ If you chose **F** the most, go to Chapter 2 **Page 33**.

CHAPTER I

So You're an Aggressive Animal

It turns out you're one tough cookie! You may not have fancied yourself a particularly aggressive person, but if you think it over for a while, we're guessing that you'll agree with this classification. You might be wondering what all this means. You might not be wondering that at all. Either way, let's talk a little about the implications of you being Mr. or Ms. Aggressive.

Just because you're a tough guy or girl doesn't necessarily mean you go around throwing fists and mouthing off. Then again, it's certainly possible that you're very familiar with those things. There are many ways for your aggressiveness to manifest itself, and we think that you'll just fall in love with the animal you turn out to be.

What happens after you take the second test? Then it's time to put up some tiger shark wallpaper on your computer's desktop! Oh, and you should also make a tiger shark T-shirt. Whatever you do, go off and be bold! We know you can do it. After all, the proof is in your survey results...

Now that you know you're an aggressive animal, take this short test to find out which specific animal you resemble most.

1. When someone hits you, do you ALWAYS hit him or her back?

○ YES   If you chose YES, go to question 2.
○ NO   If you chose NO, go to question 4.

2. Do you analyze things and think differently than many people?

○ YES   If you chose YES, go to question 3.
○ NO   If you chose NO, go to question 6.

3. How unpredictable are you? Rate yourself from 1 (predictable) to 3 (very unpredictable).

○ 1   If you chose 1, you are a GRAY WOLF.
○ 2   If you chose 2, you are a COBRA.
○ 3   If you chose 3, you are a KODIAK BEAR.

4. Are you a bit paranoid or nervous?

○ YES   If you chose YES, go to question 5.
○ NO   If you chose NO, go to question 7.

5. How intimidated do you get by others? Rate yourself from 1 (never intimidated) to 3 (often intimidated).

○ 1   If you chose 1, you are a PUMA.
○ 2   If you chose 2, you are a HYENA.
○ 3   If you chose 3, you are a COYOTE.

6. If you had to choose, do you spend more time trying to intimidate others or impress others?

○ INTIMIDATE If you chose INTIMIDATE, you are a TIGER SHARK.
○ IMPRESS   If you chose IMPRESS, you are a BETTA or SIAMESE FIGHTING FISH.

7. Are you often the underdog in fights or competitions? Rate yourself from 1 (rarely the underdog) to 3 (often the underdog).

○ 1   If you chose 1, you are a DWARF BUFFALO.
○ 2   If you chose 2, you are a WOLVERINE.
○ 3   If you chose 3, you are a SHORT-TAILED SHREW.

THE GRAY WOLF

You're tough and success-oriented. You rely on the people you trust.

- **You're tough, but you need others to help you stay tough:** Even though the gray wolf can be a fierce predator (especially the alpha male), it needs a pack of two to fifteen others to rule the wild. On the rare occasion that this wolf finds a potential meal on its own, it quickly howls for others to help out. If you're truly like the gray wolf, you're not the most independent of people.

- **Even though you can be social, you're not interested in anyone besides your closest friends:** While the gray wolf enjoys the company of the others in its pack, it *never* associates with gray wolves from other packs. Are you also the type that sticks to a few very reliable friends?

- **You're willing to look for success in many places:** While some people remain in the comfort of their usual niche, you'll go where you need to go to find fulfillment. When the gray wolf hunts for its food, it travels more often and for greater distances than virtually any other animal.

- **You're not afraid of the really big guy:** Plain and simple — a gray wolf will attack animals far larger than itself, like moose and very big caribou.

- **All of that being said, you're still not *always* up for the fight:** Does your toughness tend to wane a bit when someone else challenges your aggression? If a potential prey stands up to a gray wolf's attack, oftentimes the wolf will simply move on to an easier quarry. In addition, if this wolf fails to catch its prey within a 1,000-yard chase, it'll most likely give up.

- **You appreciate a certain consistency in your life:** Even though the gray wolf travels over great distances, it will still maintain a single den for years, which is rare for most animals. Have you ever passed on the opportunity to upgrade something simply to maintain the familiar?

- **Are you a big fan of Hillary Rodham Clinton's *It Takes A Village*?** Child-rearing is a communal activity for the gray wolf. While you probably don't have such collective efforts in your life, do you still tend to value cooperation among your close allies?

THE KODIAK BEAR

You're creative, unpredictable, and self-sufficient.

- **By no means are you Mr. or Ms. Social:** From the time they leave their mothers, Kodiak bears live on their own. They rely on their own personal toughness to get by.

- **Face it. Everyone knows you as the clumsy one:** Even though the Kodiak is one of the most aggressive bears, it moves around with a low, clumsy walk. When it stands on its legs in times of danger, the Kodiak bear obviously carries a lot more dignity.

- **You usually have lots of creative ways of ultimately getting what you want:** Kodiaks are omnivores, meaning that they're up for eating both meat and veggies. A Kodiak uses its huge jaws to catch fish, occasionally pinning them underwater with its forepaws before finally clasping them in its teeth. It'll dig insects from rotting logs and pull small mammals right out of their burrows. This bear will tackle huge animals and scoop up salmon on their way upstream. What we're trying to say is that Kodiaks have all sorts of ways for getting their prize. Are you as diverse and crafty?

- **Will you go so far as to threaten others to get your way?** A Kodiak bear stakes out territory by threatening any animal that comes in its path. It takes advantage of its enormous size, with the largest bears securing the choicest locations.

- **Does the cold weather put you in a malaise?** As soon as winter comes around, these bears become incredibly lazy. They don't hunt, they don't interact, and they don't worry about mating. While not hibernators, Kodiaks will still curl up into a light slumber, living off of their supply of fat. You're probably the type that gets a little depressed in the winter and even avoids other people.

- **You're sort of crazy — very rash and unpredictable:** Kodiak bears keep humans and other animals on their toes because they're terribly unpredictable. They're known to do anything without rhyme or reason. As the largest carnivorous land animal, these guys are not to be messed with. If you're a loose cannon capable of explosion, you've probably found your match.

THE COYOTE

You like change, you use people, and you get intimidated.

- **You are an aggressor but you often feel subject to other people's aggression:** While coyotes are hunters themselves, they're no match for bigger grizzly bears, mountain lions, black bears, and humans. Declining populations of most huge, vicious aggressors, however, have helped coyotes to survive. Nonetheless, these wild dogs have to suck up their fair share of aggression from others in the wilderness.

- **You use others to obtain your own ends:** The coyote oftentimes uses the American badger as a tool to get what it wants. While the badger digs for rodents at one end of a burrow, a coyote waits to pounce on any animals that emerge from an escape hole at the other end. The badger does the work, while the coyote sits and waits. Not the most honorable of traits.

- **You're very independent:** While some coyotes may hunt with one or two others, most tend to operate solo. Aside from a mother tending her kids, you'll rarely see coyotes together. This one's straightforward; you know whether or not you prefer being alone.

- **You move around often:** Coyotes do not have permanent homes. They roam the lands on their own, stopping to seize bounty. It should be noted, however, that coyotes appreciate their nomadic lifestyle. If you actively seek out the feeling of change and mobility, then this might be the proper match for you.

THE TIGER SHARK

You surprise and scare everyone. People respect you.

- **You're afraid of absolutely no one:** Tiger sharks are incredibly dangerous, and they rule the waters without the slightest bit of fear. They're not afraid to go anywhere in the ocean, as many have been spotted even in the most shallow of waters. These sharks are more common in warmer water, but they'll move into colder areas if they sense something they want. Tiger sharks can easily be 16 feet in length. Just think of how big eight feet is. Now multiply that by two! Pretty outrageous. Bottom line: If you're like this shark you're a huge presence, you don't take bull from anyone, and you get what you want because you can simply take it.

- **You're interested in all sorts of successes:** These sharks have been known to eat almost anything, including clothing, tin cans, bolts, wire, wood, birds, and alligator heads. Tiger sharks like the thrill of the hunt. They won't kill something if they're not hungry, but for the most part, nothing in their path is remotely safe. If you're like this ferocious animal, you look for success or riches in all places. If the opportunity knocks, you're all over it.

- **People actually fear you:** Humans greatly fear tiger sharks, and with good reason. To give you a sense of their capabilities, it's worth mentioning the famous Florida Shark-Arm case of 1944. A fisherman caught a large tiger shark near the coast, and when he gutted his prize, he found inside the shark a man's body intact from ribs to knees. This true story and many others have made the tiger shark an immense source of fear. If you're willing to call yourself a tiger shark, then you're prepared to say that almost everyone fears you.

- **Your successes tend to surprise others:** Even if a potential prey spots a tiger shark from afar, it can do little to alter its fate if the shark has made a decision to go in for the kill. Still, tiger sharks prefer areas that allow them to maximize the element of surprise. They tend to like murky waters with poor visibility, enabling them to sneak right up on their victims. To be like a tiger shark, not everyone should know about your plans of action, and your successes, while common, always intrigue others.

THE HYENA

You're educated, adaptable, and possessive.

- **Much of your success comes from your ability to adapt to the situation:** A person's success or failure often relies upon his or her willingness to change with varying circumstances. The hyena is great at sizing up the situation and acting accordingly. While they usually just use their impressive speed to kill prey, hyenas are flexible and can learn all sorts of innovative hunting techniques.

SURVIVAL SKILL #61: STEAL FOOD FROM LIONS

- **You value a good education:** While most animals do a good job of preparing their young for the wild, hyenas are especially good about passing on their knowledge. Most other animals instinctively pass on a few crucial survival methods to their young, but hyenas will pass on very specific survival tricks that they may have picked up by themselves. If you tend to pass on your discoveries to others for their benefit, you share a similarity with the hyena.

- **Perhaps you lack the best foresight:** Hyenas do not always eat the entirety of their catch. But as soon as they leave their partially-eaten prey, they forget that they even left it there. While other animals would bring this food back to a lair to be consumed later, hyenas do not have this useful foresight. If you also don't have the best memory, you're not unlike the hyena.

- **You rely upon a tight community:** Hyenas live in communities of about 40, and break up into small groups when they go out hunting. A greeting ceremony allows hyenas to recognize members of their own clans.

- **You label everything you own with a marker:** Hyenas don't like other animals hanging around territory they deem their own. They mark their space by secreting a smelly liquid known as "hyena butter." If you secrete bodily liquid all over your CDs, you've got what it takes to be a hyena. If you're just protective of your belongings, that also counts.

- **You're the type that has long-standing rivalries:** Hyenas and lions hate each other. Lions will kill hyenas without provocation, and hyenas will do the same to lionesses.

THE SHORT-TAILED SHREW

You're tough for your size, you're unhygienic, and you get things done.

- **You're much more aggressive than your size would ever suggest:** Short-tailed shrews are only about 80mm long, but they'll attack all sorts of larger animals including frogs, salamanders, snakes, birds, mice, and other shrews. These short-tailed shrews have glands that secrete a toxic material that they use to subdue their prey. If the short-tailed shrew does not get food every two hours, it will try to eat other short-tailed shrews! If you're known as the tough little guy or gal, this is probably your match.

- **You like to be left alone:** For the most part, short-tailed shrews are solitary animals. They like to be left alone to find food, and they're quick to get in fights with their own kind.

- **You don't care much about your personal hygiene, which tends to displease others:** These shrews usually have a very foul odor because of their toxic secretion, which can keep potential predators away. If you deliberately abstain from making yourself presentable in order to keep people at a distance, you may share something in common with the short-tailed shrew.

- **You believe in a solid work ethic:** If you value hard work, you have something else in common with the short-tailed shrew. It expends lots of energy constructing elaborate runways under leaves, dirt, and snow and building nests in tunnels or under logs and rocks.

THE PUMA

You plan well and command power, but you're paranoid.

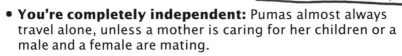

- **You command a certain respect wherever you go:** A puma walks with a unique grace and dignity fitting for such a strong predator. It has incredibly powerful limbs that enable it to jump to heights of 18 feet or more, and its climbing abilities are extraordinary. If you don't command respect for your strength and grace, you should probably move on to another animal.

- **You're completely independent:** Pumas almost always travel alone, unless a mother is caring for her children or a male and a female are mating.

- **You like to carefully plan things out:** Pumas are known as "stalking predators" rather than "pursuit predators." They use their intelligence to pick out prime sniper positions and to time their attacks perfectly. Whereas the hyena devotes most of its effort to the chase, the puma focuses on the planning.

- **Not to mention your unique patience:** When the puma stakes out a position from which to attack its prey, it can remain there for long periods of time — until the moment is perfect. You need this trait if you're going to call yourself a puma.

- **You have certain irrational fears:** If pumas hear the bark of any dog (even a very small one), they get terribly scared and run away. Aside from humans, pumas have virtually no predators, so why the overreaction? Some scientists believe that somewhere in the puma's evolutionary past, it must have been preyed upon by some sort of barking animal. You should know whether or not you have these kinds of senseless fears.

THE COBRA

You're vicious, vindictive, and image-conscious.

- **You're pretty introverted, but when riled up you're vicious:** These snakes are seldom seen and for the most part, they tend to be shy. But when they're angered, they can bite with a frightening unpredictability. To make matters worse, they have the capability of atomizing venom accurately to a distance of up to 20 feet. If you get bitten by a cobra, expect some major amputation or even death. Bottom line: These guys aren't running around looking for trouble, but if you get on their bad side, you're likely to lose a limb.

- **You rub salt in people's wounds:** When cobras seize an animal, they chew on it for a while to inject even more poison. Even when the prey or enemy is dead, the cobra will continue chewing and injecting. Are you not satisfied with winning a fight or argument? Do you insist on taking it one level further by rubbing salt in the wounds?

- **You wear clothing that makes you look tough:** When cobras get nervous or anxious, they move their ribs in order to flatten their necks. This movement creates the appearance of a "hood" on the cobra's head. When other animals see the hood, they know the cobra is angry and trouble may ensue. Anyone who has ever seen the cobra's hood knows how intimidating it can be. Do you dress and carry yourself in a manner that intimidates other people?

- **You lift weights or at least work out to get big and strong:** When cobras get angry, not only do they form hoods, but they also stand up straight to intimidate potential enemies. In fact, snake charmers don't really "charm" cobras into standing up. They're just nervous and on-guard. If you take active measures to build your body, or at least to look strong, you're like the cobra.

THE DWARF BUFFALO

You're sociable and strong but also irritable.

- **You're a pretty social person:** These buffalo travel in herds of up to one thousand. And they're all best friends. They help each other avoid attacks from predators, and they're extremely loyal to the herd. To be like a dwarf buffalo, you need to be tough, social, and principled.

- **You love a sweet revenge:** Many brave tribal hunters fear the dwarf buffalo because it has been known to return at night to avenge the killing of its kin. When angry, these animals have been known to destroy crops and homes.

- **You have a very short temper:** While a dwarf buffalo does not charge at every animal that comes into its path, they are easily provoked and angered. Most animals are no match for this huge beast. They ram their horns and hooves into their enemy, before rolling their quarter-ton bodies over the victim to top things off.

- **No one uses you for his or her own purposes:** Because of the ferocity of the dwarf buffalo, humans have never been able to domesticate it. If you're like this animal, people know not to play games with you.

THE WOLVERINE

You're an instigator and you feel entitled to things, but you're a survivor.

- **You're a natural born survivor. You overcome every hardship:** Wolverines are hard-working, tough survivors.

They have very strong muscles, claws, teeth, and jaws, and their endurance is excellent. Naturalists have seen these mammals kill and drag 120-pound sheep for two miles across all sorts of terrain! Do you step up to big challenges to survive or get ahead?

- **You'll pick fights with anyone:** Wolverines are not afraid of anything. Hunters have reported wolverines driving Kodiak bears and wolves from carcasses! They're vicious and aggressive and far stronger than their 30-pound bodies suggest.

- **You've been denied certain things in your life, so now you feel entitled to more:** Wolverines often go for long periods of time without any food. But they chow down like crazy when they get ahold of some grub. Not only are they smart enough to store up fat (hence their survival skills), but they feel entitled to a feast after enduring a famine. Do you feel that you deserve more to compensate for having had less?

- **When you're in a bad mood, you often take it out on others. You're not afraid to tick people off:** Sometimes hungry wolverines break into uninhabited cabins and wreak absolute havoc. They make a huge mess and intentionally release a horribly offensive odor (out of habit), earning them the nickname "devil bears." If you're hungry, unfulfilled, or just plain angry, do you ever take it out on other people? When you're in a bad mood, do others end up suffering?

THE BETTA OR SIAMESE FIGHTING FISH

You can't get along with people and you like to showboat.

- **You're misanthropic and nasty:** Siamese fighting fish just can't get along with one another. In fact, if you put two males in one fish bowl, they'll fight to the death. Females are almost as aggressive as males, but they usually calm down after one demonstrates superiority. Siamese fighting fish are extremely territorial, and even males and females will constantly chase and bite each other. They'll even fight their reflections in mirrors! If you're like this aggressive fish, you don't care about community or friendship. You're skeptical of others, and you're a pretty nasty person.

- **You like to show off, but only in your small niche. You're the big-fish-in-a-small-pond type:** Siamese fighting fish are absolutely beautiful. They have vibrant colors, and some have long, swaying fins. But they live in very small, modest territories. In the natural environment, you can find them in small puddles in paddy fields. In pet stores, they're ordinarily kept in small fish bowls. These beautiful fish flaunt their attractiveness, but only in an unaesthetic environment. If you like being a big fish in a small pond, you're similar to the Siamese fighting fish.

- **You like physical comforts:** When Siamese fighting fish are content, they make a bubble nest for themselves. By blowing these bubbles, they express satisfaction as well as preparedness for mating. If you're like these fish, you can be mean and grumpy, but you're satisfied when you have nice things and a comfortable environment.

- **You get beet red when you're angry:** When Siamese fighting fish are angry or preparing for attack, they become colored with more vibrant reds, greens, blues, and purples. Do you get so enraged sometimes that your face gets bright red? Do you show other physical signs of anger easily?

CHAPTER 2

So You're an Industrious Animal

Well, it looks like we have a hard worker in the room! You probably spend a lot of time at your desk and not so much time outside by the playground. Maybe you've got the industrious spirit in your blood or maybe you just know that hard work pays off. Either way, you tend to be an industrious person, and it's about time you started *working* on the second personality test!

You may still have reservations about your classification into this particular category. While it's always possible that you belong elsewhere, you should also recognize that many of us lack a relative conception of our own work ethic and capacity. In other words, you might work harder than most people and just not realize it.

It's also worth mentioning that very few animals in the wilderness are actually lazy. In fact, most devote their full life's effort to survival and procreation. The animals in this section, however, show an *extraordinary* tendency to work hard. Some of them do it with a proverbial smile and others do it with a proverbial shotgun. Some are shy and some are bold. Some are birds and some are not birds.

But enough babble talk. Any minute someone could ask you what animal you're like, and you wouldn't even know the answer! Get crackin'!

Now that you know you're an industrious animal, take this short test to find out which specific animal you resemble most.

1. Do you constantly work hard specifically to improve your life?

○ YES   If you chose YES, go to question 2.
○ NO   If you chose NO, go to question 5.

2. Do you work particularly well with others?

○ YES   If you chose YES, go to question 3.
○ NO   If you chose NO, go to question 4.

3. How much do you like riches and extravagant things? Rate yourself from 1 (not especially) to 3 (very much).

○ 1   If you chose 1, you are a LEAF-CUTTING ANT.
○ 2   If you chose 2, you are a PIKA.
○ 3   If you chose 3, you are a BEAVER.

4. Are you very socially conscious?

○ YES   If you chose YES, you are a GOPHER TORTOISE.
○ NO   If you chose NO, you are a TASMANIAN DEVIL.

5. Can you honestly say that you *always* strive for excellence?

○ YES   If you chose YES, go to question 6.
○ NO   If you chose NO, go to question 7.

6. How often do you strive to do things that seem impossible? Rate yourself from 1 (not very often) to 3 (very often).

○ 1   If you chose 1, you are a CLAM.
○ 2   If you chose 2, you are a CARPENTER BEE.
○ 3   If you chose 3, you are a GOLDEN PLOVER.

7. How routine is your daily lifestyle? Rate yourself from 1 (not very routine) to 3 (very routine).

○ 1   If you chose 1, you are a MULE.
○ 2   If you chose 2, you are a PORCUPINE.
○ 3   If you chose 3, you are a MOLE.

THE PIKA

You like your niche and you look to the future. You communicate well.

- **You ensure a stable future for yourself:** Pikas don't hibernate during the winter but instead gather lots of food to carry them through the cold. They fill their mouths with different types of plants, each carefully arranged crosswise, which they artfully craft into neat piles at home. These preparations require physical and mental toughness, and most importantly, a willingness to endure. People who are like pikas work hard in the present for their well-being in the future.

- **You hate to be out of your comfort zone:** While pikas can tolerate a very cold climate, they die immediately if their temperatures go slightly above or below the norm. For that reason, you'll never see pikas anywhere but in the high country. Do you think you would also be unable to handle a big move from one locale to another?

- **You communicate well with others:** The pika actually gets its name from its high-pitched "peeeeek" sound, which allows for good communication with others. Mountain observers note that the loud pika call seems to come from all directions at once. So pika-like people are certainly not afraid to be vocal.

- **Nonetheless, you know when to shut up:** As loud as pikas are, they know to be dead silent to avoid predators. While some vocal people never stop their chitter-chatter, you have a good sense of when and where not to pipe up.

THE BEAVER

You work harder than anyone to keep improving your life, and you accept help graciously.

- **You are the king of hard work. No one tops you:** No animal works quite as hard as the beaver. It's constantly gathering food, cutting down trees, and building protective fortresses for itself. Beavers' bodies are designed to do heavy labor in the water. When they submerge themselves in rivers, their nose and ear valves close off so that no water gets in while they work. And they use their tail as a fifth leg for extra support. These animals are truly the most dedicated, tireless creatures on the planet. If you deem yourself a beaver, you're making a big statement.

- **You welcome help from others, but you never rely upon it:** Beavers often build dams to insure a minimum water level, and sometimes they'll work with others to make it happen. But these steadfast animals are more than willing to do the job on their own. If you appreciate help but know not to depend too heavily on it, you share something important with the beaver.

- **You don't mind upgrading your lifestyle when you earn more money:** Each year the beaver adds more complexity and stability to its den, in addition to any necessary repairs. These additions are something of a luxury for the beaver, representing the fruits of its hard labor in the forest. Are you the type that might upgrade your car after a jumbo pay bonus?

- **People often compliment your perfume:** Glands at the base of the beaver's tail release castor, a strong-smelling, oily substance attractive to many animals. While this natural essence attracts other beavers for mating, it can also help predators locate their beaver prey.

- **You have a skill for landscape architecture:** Not only do beavers build elaborate dens and dams, but they also build underwater food pantries. When a beaver wants to tap into its food supply, it swims down to one of these caches and brings the contents back to the den. While beaver-like people don't need to have landscape architectural skills, consider them a bonus similarity if you do.

THE LEAF-CUTTING ANT

You're intimate, stable, and socially conscious.

- **You radiate intimacy:** Leaf-cutting ants release pheromones to communicate business and mating information. Similarly, some people don't even have to open their mouths to express their desires and thoughts to other people. Think it over.

- **You value the efficiency of modern industrialism:** These ants have a clearly defined division of labor in their societies. The smallest ants remain in the nest and serve as gardeners and nursemaids. Medium-sized ants search for leaves, which they cut up and bring back to the nest. They also help out with some of the important housekeeping duties. The largest ants serve as soldiers, protecting the colony and overseeing the proper disposal of waste. Some people think that the division of labor in society creates disillusionment, but if you like this organizational structure, you're not unlike the leaf-cutting ant.

- **You'd rather make it than buy it:** Leaf-cutting ants thrive on fungus, but they don't look for it in the wild. Instead, they use their own compost heaps to grow fungus inside their nests.

- **You detest discrimination:** Gender plays no part in the social roles of leaf-cutting ants. Females can work as gardeners, gatherers, or soldiers alongside the males. How much do you think about issues of gender equality?

THE GOPHER TORTOISE

You're kind, and your work helps others.

- **Your hard work is very important to others:** Gopher tortoises live in burrows, which they dig incessantly. Although one burrow serves as a primary residence, the gopher tortoise usually maintains many others. As they outgrow certain burrows, however, other animals such as the eastern indigo snake, the eastern diamondback rattlesnake, and the gopher frog take over residence inside these deep and safe shelters. The industriousness of these tortoises is therefore very important to other wildlife. Do you sometimes work for others' benefits?

- **Others sometimes take advantage of your good nature:** Gopher tortoises are so unthreatening that they often have to worry about small, relatively weak predators such as raccoons, gray foxes, striped skunks, armadillos, dogs, snakes, and raptors. Even tiny fire ants have been known to prey upon gopher tortoise hatchlings. Unfortunately, these tortoises end up creating homes for the very animals that kill them for food. Do you ever feel mistreated by the people you help every day?

- **You work hard but you're not in a rush:** Gopher tortoises can live for up to 100 years, so it's no surprise that they don't feel pressure to live life in the fast lane. While these tortoises move around a sizable amount (they can roam around areas about eight acres large), they take their precious time to do it. You'll probably live as long as one of these tortoises, but do you have the same relaxed attitude?

INDUSTRIOUS

THE TASMANIAN DEVIL

You're not picky, but you always want more.

- **You'll take what you can get:** Tasmanian devils eat mostly dead animals on the sides of roads. They have voracious appetites, so they'll pretty much take whatever they can get their hands on.

- **You're never fully satisfied:** Since Tasmanian devils can eat almost 40 percent of their own body weight in less than 30 minutes, they'll never turn down an opportunity for some food. They'll hang around farmlands, where the chance of finding carrion is pretty high. For the most part, Tasmanian devils are never satisfied.

- **Sometimes you like to impress audiences with your double-jointed tricks:** Not unlike your potential trick thumb, the Tasmanian devil has incredible jaw capabilities. Its jaw is nine times more powerful than a dog's, and can open to form a 180-degree angle! You don't need impressive body tricks to be like this animal, but if you have them, you're on the right path.

- **You're not the most social person:** Tasmanian devils tend to be pretty shy. They hunt at night, usually alone, and they most often avoid conflict with other animals. Occasionally they'll attack a young or wounded animal as they let out a demonic cry, but usually they'll just stick with carrion. If you resemble this dog-like animal, you tend to be pretty timid overall.

THE CLAM

Your hard work hurts others around you. You strive for quality.

- **You work hard, but it harms a lot of people:** Clams slowly but consistently erode rocky reefs. They scrape away at the soft rock, burrowing a foot or more deep. The rasping weakens reefs so severely that they crumble with the onset of winter storms. So even though these clams try to burrow for their own well-being, they harm many other animals in the process. Does your work help you but hurt others?

- **Still, your work is an asset to a small group:** Clams are actually very valuable to people. They're a precious but diminishing source of food enjoyed by many cultures. For Native Americans in the past, clams held even more value. They used hard-shell clams, or "quahog," for money, or "wampum." Even though your work hurts some people, does it benefit a small group of others?

- **You absorb a lot of information, but you know how to sort the important from the unimportant:** Clams have two rear openings called siphons, which take in water filled with food and oxygen. The clam gives off carbon dioxide from the oxygen, and its gill hairs sweep food into a small mouth and stomach. Everything that is deemed useless is sent back out into the water. Clams take in a lot, keep the useful stuff, and get rid of the trash. Are you good at filtering out nonsense from useful information?

- **You look exactly your age; not younger, not older:** Clams have growth lines on their shells, indicating their age, not unlike the age-telling rings on a cross-section of a tree trunk. The mantle, a fleshy part of the clam's body, secretes a substance that forms the shell both for natural growth as well as repair. Do you look your age? If so, you're similar to the clam.

THE GOLDEN PLOVER

You're courageously determined to accomplish the impossible.

- **You step up to seemingly impossible challenges:** Pacific golden plovers hold the world record for the longest nonstop flight. They migrate from their homes in the Arctic Circle all the way to Hawaii or the Polynesian Islands. They go without food or water for thousands of miles, and then must land on islands barely visible from the sky. Truly a remarkable feat.

- **You are quite the courageous one:** The elder golden plovers head south earlier than the younger birds, who need more time to bulk up before the big trip. Many of the

youngest golden plovers find their way without ever having traveled before and without the help of a leader. These amazing birds not only work hard but also show tremendous courage.

- **Your work excites you:** When the golden plover searches for food, it darts a few steps forward on its legs, pokes around for a snail or an insect, then darts off again to another spot. People who are like golden plovers show great energy and enthusiasm for their work.

- **Your responsible lifestyle keeps you looking great:** You may have to shed a little modesty here and acknowledge that you're one great-looking person. At the end of every year, golden plovers shed some of their old feathers and grow new ones with different colors. With their long legs and graceful posture, these birds seem very proud of their super looks.

- **Even though you value hard work, you'll fake sickness here and there:** While golden plovers sometimes defend themselves by charging at enemies and screeching, they'll often just pretend to be hurt or dead to avoid dangerous conflict. The point is, you'll do what you need to do to get some rest now and then.

THE PORCUPINE

You're calm and focused. You work to provide yourself with a nice life.

- **You have a calm, consistent composure:** Porcupines are very relaxed animals. If a potential enemy approaches, they simply gnash their teeth and shake their tails, but they always remain calm. They swim easily, and they enjoy grazing on plants in shallow water. Do you have a good, relaxed grip on your emotions and reactions?

- **You're not defenseless, but you always avoid a fight:** If you know how to stand up for yourself, but you still hate fighting, you're very similar to the porcupine. When this animal needs to protect itself, it uses its tail to throw its quills at the enemy. Once the barbed quills penetrate an animal's skin, they're terribly difficult and painful to remove. In fact, the more the animal moves around, the deeper the quills go. But despite the porcupine's weaponry, it absolutely hates to fight. It'll climb trees or run away to avoid a conflict with another animal. Do you hate conflict?

- **You work hard primarily so you can afford the things you like:** Porcupines eat plants and flowers, but during the winter, they work harder as they eat the cambium layer of tree trunks. Trees send sugar to gnawed portions of the bark, which attracts the porcupine to that same sugary spot over and over again. As you can imagine, this doesn't do wonders for the tree's well-being. In addition, porcupines lack salt in their diets, so they love to get ahold of it. They're known to chew on the sweaty boots and clothing of hikers. All in all, these animals like to indulge, but they know they've got to work to make it possible. Do you work hard to provide yourself with certain luxuries?

- **Your weaknesses are apparent to others:** A porcupine's quills offer some protection, but enemies are well-aware of this animal's weaknesses. Porcupines do not have quills on their bellies, so predators like wolverines, bears, wolves, lynxes, foxes, coyotes, and owls can knock the porcupine on its back and go in for the kill. If your weaknesses are pretty obvious to other people, you have at least a little porcupine in you.

INDUSTRIOUS

THE MULE

You can endure almost anything, but you know your limitations.

- **You can endure tough working conditions:** As a hybrid offspring of a horse and a donkey, mules tend to acquire the best traits of both animals. Mules can endure extreme temperatures, travel rugged terrain, and survive on very meager food rations. These abilities make them great for carrying cargo and doing all sorts of farm work. If you have a knack for bearing bad conditions or fighting through unpleasant jobs, you're certainly a mule person.

- **You're more talented than either of your parents:** The capacity of mules far exceeds their horse and donkey parents. Mules are stronger, live longer, grow taller, suffer wounds less frequently, and have better stamina. While many children have talents that their parents lack, mules bring it to the extreme. Are you clearly more talented than Mom and Dad?

- **You push yourself to the max, but you're smart about not overdoing it:** Even though mules work very hard, they're very smart about not overexerting themselves. In fact, their notorious stubbornness comes from their refusal to do overly dangerous work. While these constant efforts at self-preservation can be frustrating to industrious owners, they actually help insure the safety of the human and his cargo. If you're the type who makes sure to drink extra water on hot days, stretch before physical activity, and take needed breaks here and there, you're very similar to the mule. Mules work hard, but they won't make themselves sick and crazy because of it.

- **You might sacrifice family time because of your work:** Mules are not family-oriented animals. Even though they have sexual urges like other animals, they're an infertile breed. A few mule offspring have been *reported*, but as of now, we don't believe they can actually reproduce. That means no kids and no proper family. Do you miss out on family time because you work so hard?

- **You do your work with grace, and you make it look easy:** Not only can mules do an impressive amount of hard labor, they even make it look easy. These large, strong animals actually walk on their tiptoes! Perhaps they don't have quite the grace of a ballerina, but given all of the trekking and carrying they do with seeming ease, these tip-toers make the job look easy through their natural grace. Do you make difficult work seem easy because of your talents and unique abilities?

THE MOLE

You're a good, hard-working, honest, routine person.

- **You're not an outdoors person. You work hard indoors all day long:** Few people ever get the chance to see moles because they spend all their time digging underground. Once in a while, people can see them pushing up ridges in the grass, but that's about it. In fact, their little eyeballs are entirely covered in skin to protect them from the dirt. If you're like the mole, you spend all your time inside, and you rarely see the light of day. At the very least, you'd prefer to be indoors most of the time.

- **You don't mind long, methodical tasks:** Moles are designed for digging. They do it all the time. Their torpedo-shaped bodies, cone-shaped heads, and pointy noses are perfect for "swimming" through the dirt underground. They have short, hairless tails that help guide their movement, powerful shoulders and forearms, shovel-like paws, and powerful claws. Moles perform a "breaststroke" through the soil as they diligently search for food. In the winter they dig deeper, pushing the displaced soil up onto the ground, which forms mole hills. It's obvious that with all their digging, these little rodents are especially tough workers. Do you have it in you to do tiresome, rigorous, repetitive work every single day?

- **You like to enjoy the good life:** Moles *love* to eat. Some even eat the equivalent of their own weight in just one day! They hunt for white grubs, earthworms, wireworms, cutworms, and other insects, and they also eat some plant material here and there. They suck up the earthworms like spaghetti, and they pin insects against burrow walls until they can finish the deed with their sharp teeth. Moles are

INDUSTRIOUS

often blamed for enjoying the good life a little too much. Farmers blame them for damaging bulbs and garden crops, even though mice are usually at fault for these invasions. Mole people love to indulge. They work hard, but they certainly like to enjoy themselves.

- **You're sort of a loner:** Even though moles sometimes bump into each other underground, they tend to completely avoid real interaction. In fact, if two moles are confined together, they'll fight to the death! They're not terribly aggressive animals, they just like to be alone. If you don't like chit-chat or spending much time with others, you may be a mole person.

- **You like your work to make a difference in people's lives:** Even though many people complain that moles damage lawns and golf courses, they do a great service by eliminating all sorts of insects. In addition to that, all their digging and tunneling shifts the soil so it can conserve more water. So all in all, the hard work of these rodents does the world a ton of good. Do you hope that your work helps other people's lives?

THE CARPENTER BEE

You're creative, messy, and diligent.

- **You love making things rather than buying them:**
Carpenter bees use creative tactics and hard work to
survive. When carpenter bees are ready to lay eggs, they
drill holes or cells in wood, which they line with "bee
bread," a combination of pollen and regurgitated nectar
that cushions and nourishes the eggs. When carpenter bees
drill wood, you can actually hear the drilling sound as they
labor away. It takes them six full days just to drill one inch
of wood! Once they finish making the cell, which includes
tunnels and galleries, they seal it up, providing safety for
their unhatched eggs. If you like creating, building, and
getting things done without calling for professional help,
you're like the carpenter bee.

- **You like to fix up old things to make them look new:**
Carpenter bees are great at refurbishing their homes. They
nest in the same areas for generations, fixing up old holes
and expanding tunnels and burrows. Of course, they'll
often start from scratch, but they're definitely good at
remodeling and renovating. Do you enjoy turning a mess
into something nice? Do you like to upgrade your things a
little every year?

- **You sometimes get a bad reputation from the people
you spend time with:** Many people are afraid of buzzing
carpenter bees, but most don't even sting at all. First,
males don't even have stingers, so they're not dangerous
at all; and second, females almost never sting people,
though they do have stingers. That's not to say that
carpenter bees are not pests; they bore through wooden
water tanks and houses, they stain wood by defecating on
it, and their buzzing and invasiveness can be irritating to
people. Nonetheless, the carpenter bee gets a bad rap
about stinging because of other bee species. Do you often
find yourself deemed guilty by association?

- **You don't take great care of the nice things you
own:** Even though carpenter bees create very nice nests in
houses, structural timbers, water tanks, and fences, they
insist on defecating right on the outside of their entrances.
That means that every time they enter their homes, they

INDUSTRIOUS

have to look at their excrement. Do you tend to make a mess easily? Could you stand to take better care of your things?

- **Even though you're a very hard worker, you go through periods of laziness:** Carpenter bees work incredibly hard during the warm weather, but they hibernate in their holes over the winter. Since the eggs have already been laid, the bees just wait until the cold passes to resume their industrious activity. If you go through periods where you have difficulty motivating yourself despite your inherent industriousness, you might be a carpenter bee person.

CHAPTER 3

So You're a Sneaky Animal

Well, you might be a little disappointed right now. You thought you were the industrious type — maybe even curious — but it turns out you're one sneaky person. Whether you like it or not, people can't trust you very much. We're guessing that you always try to get ahead, and you'll step on pretty much anyone along the way. And as if that weren't bad enough, you're manipulative and selfish!

Okay. Maybe we're taking this a little too far, but that doesn't change the fact that you're still one sneaky individual. Sneaky people can also have some redeeming qualities; they're often smart, innovative, and successful. They may not be the most well-liked, but they're usually one step ahead of everyone else. Unfortunately, these sneaky types usually use their endowments to serve themselves and no one else.

As you flip through this chapter, you'll come across a bunch of different sneaky animals — some more conniving than others. Whether you're more clever than selfish or more ambitious than manipulative, the second test should match you up very well. But make sure to be honest when answering the questions! We'd all love to be clever, benevolent, and respected, but it's just not that easy. So if you can keep it within that sneaky mind of yours, try to be true to yourself as we continue. Good luck...

Now that you know you're a sneaky animal, take this short test to find out which specific animal you resemble most.

1. Are you a very outgoing person?

○ YES   If you chose YES, go to question 2.
○ NO   If you chose NO, go to question 5.

2. Do you have a tendency to attract animosity?

○ YES   If you chose YES, go to question 3.
○ NO   If you chose NO, go to question 4.

3. How much do you hurt other people? Rate yourself from 1 (not too much) to 3 (very much).

○ 1   If you chose 1, you are a DINGO.
○ 2   If you chose 2, you are a BUSH PIG.
○ 3   If you chose 3, you are a BACTERIUM.

4. Are you very self-conscious?

○ YES   If you chose YES, you are a BABOON.
○ NO   If you chose NO, you are an ANGLER FISH.

5. Do you always find a way to get what you want?

○ YES   If you chose YES, go to question 6.
○ NO   If you chose NO, go to question 7.

6. Are you sometimes a head case?

○ YES   If you chose YES, you are a RACCOON.
○ NO   If you chose NO, you are a WILD RAT.

7. Do you like having responsibilities?

○ YES   If you chose YES, you are a PHASMID or STICK INSECT.
○ NO   If you chose NO, you are an OPPOSUM.

THE OPOSSUM

You're shy, and you don't like responsibility.

- **You avoid responsibility by acting incapable:** In order to defend themselves from predators, opossums will pretend to be dead by slowing down their heartbeats. Once the bigger animal loses interest, opossums will wake themselves up again and continue moving around. They'll also release a horrible-smelling odor to keep others away. Some pretty sneaky stuff, you've got to admit.

- **You're quick to adapt to your surroundings:** Opossums have an uncanny ability to endure in any environment. While they prefer woodlands near the water, you'll also see them living off of scraps in cities. They're not too particular about their diet, which includes grass, mushrooms, chickens, insects, birds' eggs, fruits, garbage, and even poisonous snakes. These small animals are truly survivors. Are you also capable of getting by in almost any situation and in almost any location?

- **Even though you're sneaky, you tend to be timid:** Opossums are easily frightened by humans and other large predators despite their survival strengths. So if you're like an opossum, others have trouble keeping you down, even though you're somewhat shy.

- **You're known to pick on the industrious types:** While not a very aggressive species, the opossum kills tons of hard-working insects. Farmers often complain that opossums sneak into their chicken pens, and these animals also rid crops of lots of insects. People who are like opossums sometimes attack hard workers for their own gain or just out of sheer jealousy.

BACTERIA

People dislike you because you hurt them, but you always persevere.

- **You're completely incorrigible:** Most bacteria are widely despised by humans. Not only are they terribly harmful to people, they're also great at resisting most medicines. Did you know that over 90 percent of *Staphylococcus aureus* are now penicillin-resistant? More and more strains of bacteria can survive antibiotics, which goes to show how sneaky these creatures are.

- **No one seems to like you much:** Some bacteria can help humans digest food and maintain proper chemical balances, but overall, people aren't looking to befriend these microscopic hazards. If you're at all like bacteria, you probably haven't been invited to too many sleepovers/dinners/parties recently.

- **When people aren't trying to get rid of you, they'll just ignore your presence:** Even though people actively try to kill bacteria, many scientists believe that people aren't giving enough attention to all the new strains that are resistant to antibiotics. If you're like bacteria, others either try to squelch you or they'll just leave you alone. Either way, you don't have too many big fans.

- **Even when you're knocked down, you'll bounce back in full force:** Many people take antibiotics until they think they've killed off these harmful creatures, but oftentimes if humans stop taking medicine a bit too early, the bacteria can grow back tougher than ever. They have an unbelievable ability to bounce back from attack with incredible strength. If you're a fighter by nature, you're not unlike a dish of contemptible bacteria.

SNEAKY

THE ANGLER FISH

You're needy, controlling, and fake.

- **You pretend to be everyone's best friend:** The angler fish uses all sorts of physical signs to lure its prey. While most other predators hide and then attack, the angler fish actually manages to bring its potential victims right over to the dinner table.

...AND I'M ALSO THE RIGHTFUL KING OF PAKISTAN.

- **You're full of lies:** The angler fish attracts small fish by using a worm-like fleshy fin on its back. Not only does it look like a worm, but the angler fish even makes it look detached from the rest of his body. On top of that, the angler fish looks like nothing more than a bunch of weeds growing out of a lump of coral. If you're a compulsive liar, you're probably just like the angler fish.

- **In order to be the best, you'll move away from the competition:** Angler fish inhabit the inhospitable ocean floor, where they can catch fish without too much competition from other sea predators. You could call them "big fish in a small pond," so to speak. Do you associate with a certain crowd simply because it allows you power?

WOW...

- **You'll try to control people more powerful than you are:** Since angler fish have such large mouths, they're able to swallow prey much larger than themselves — and without much effort.

- **You can be very needy (or sympathetic to the needy):** Angler fish have a sexual dimorphism, which creates an interesting dynamic between males and females. The males, which are very small relative to the females, live as permanent parasites on the females. The male attaches himself by biting the body of the female, which connects the blood streams of the two fish. Throughout the male's dependency, he slowly degenerates, losing most of his body mass. By the end, he becomes nothing more than a source of sperm for the female. If you're like the angler fish, you're not averse to using others, and you might even allow others to use you. Your sneakiness may be a function of underlying insecurities that make you vulnerable to others.

THE RACCOON

You're smart, obsessive, and depressive.

- **You're a bit compulsive:** Raccoons always wash their food before they eat it. Virtually no other animal feels compelled to undergo this pre-dining ritual. Why do they even bother? No one knows for sure. If you have lots of little habits and exercises that you'll never abandon for a moment, you have something in common with this sneaky animal.

- **You get depressed when things aren't going well:** Even though raccoons don't hibernate, they can remain in a slumber for weeks at a time if food is scarce or the weather is too harsh.

- **You work best at night:** Raccoons are nocturnal, meaning they sleep during the day and search for food at night. If you see a raccoon walking around during daylight, there's a good chance it has rabies or some other illness. You know your work habits. Do you operate on caffeine and disregard conventional timetables?

- **You want everything and you'll take anything:** Not only are raccoons omnivorous, they'll eat just about anything at their disposal. They're incredibly resourceful

SNEAKY

animals; they'll open up trash cans and find ways into people's houses. Their sneaky ways have earned them a less than stellar reputation among suburbanites. If you want everything in sight and you'll do whatever it takes to get it, you're very similar to the raccoon.

- **You're very crafty and intelligent:** Raccoons use their front paws like hands, and they're just as comfortable in the water as they are on land. They're not the best at catching fish (they just reach in the water and grab them), but relative to most land mammals, they do a respectable job. Raccoons are also great at defending themselves. So just because you're a sneaky person doesn't mean you entirely lack good qualities. If you're like a raccoon, you have some positive talents.

THE BABOON

You're sneaky in your love life and you're self-conscious, but you're flexible.

- **You worry about others' high expectations of you:** Leaders of baboon tribes have a difficult time stepping down from their posts when they've had enough. When some elderly baboons attempt to pass on the crown of leadership, they're met with violence from the rest of the tribe.

- **You're very flexible:** Baboons will eat almost anything. They hunt antelope, gather fruits, and harvest waterlillies. Baboons are very adaptable to environmental changes, which has helped them survive the challenges imposed by man.

- **You're particularly sneaky about your love life:** Baboons tend to live in one-male groups where females spend long periods grooming the male. Even though other

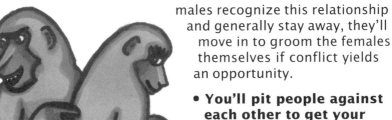

males recognize this relationship and generally stay away, they'll move in to groom the females themselves if conflict yields an opportunity.

- **You'll pit people against each other to get your way:** Some male baboons try to stir up conflict between a consorting couple so that they can have the female themselves. If you have this competitive, conniving spirit at your core, consider yourself a baboon.

- **You're essentially fearless:** Not only can baboons be vicious towards other animals, they're bold enough to walk up to tourist sites for potential bounty. Baboons also raid farmers' crops, and since humans are usually afraid to get near them, they enjoy a high rate of success. If you don't back down from anyone and you evoke fear in others, you share something else in common with the baboon.

- **You're selfish down to the core:** Baboons refuse to share the meat they catch. No exceptions. It's that simple. They feed themselves, and if anyone else wants to partake of the catch, they can do so only through very cunning tactics.

THE WILD RAT

You love some people and you hate some people. You get what you want.

- **You get along with your friends pretty well:** While wild rats know how to get what they want and how to defend themselves, they rarely fight with any of the hundred other rats in their tribe.

- **But you have no tolerance for people you don't like:** If a wild rat senses an intruder from another tribe, its territorial instincts kick in. But all wild rats maintain common military values; they'll only attack full-grown males, always sparing females and children. People like wild rats can be cunning and tough as nails, but they know when to turn it off.

- **Even though sometimes you lose your temper, you rarely pick fights:** Even though wild rats can claw enemies from time to time, they will *never* initiate a physical fight. These animals are tough, and they don't want enemies messing around with their homes and families. But when they wander from the nest, they're not looking for any serious trouble. Call yourself a wild rat if you're pretty defensive but not terribly confrontational.

- **You're very intelligent, which helps you get what you want:** Rats are a pretty capable bunch; they're stronger than cats and smarter than dogs. They're good at finding food, evading danger, and maintaining large, thriving families.

- **You take what you can get:** Wild rats have no choice but to happily accept any food they can scrounge up for themselves. They move stealthily and purposefully, which adds to their sneakiness. With humans as their greatest enemy, these smart animals have to use every ounce of strength and brains to outdo the smartest animal on earth.

THE BUSH PIG

You collude with your pals and you're greedy.

- **You're so sneaky that everyone knows to just stay away:** Bush pigs have virtually no enemies in their native Africa. They go where they want, when they want. But it's their clever sneakiness more than brute strength that wins them bounties.

- **You're terribly greedy. You want absolutely everything:** These large, sneaky pigs will eat literally everything they can get their hooves on — pineapples, grains, grapes, watermelon, and even an entire chicken or lamb. They won't hesitate to kill and devour dogs or entire cattle! Not the most admirable of traits, but one that you certainly might have.

- **You scheme in cahoots with a few of your buddies:** All bush pigs travel with four or five others, not for protection but for hunting success. They're not social animals, but they know that having each other around will allow for more spoils. If you're like a bush pig, you don't really like other people, but you might use them for your own needs.

- **If someone poses an obstacle, you'll just get even more sneaky:** Bush pigs have no trouble at all breaking down fences and digging under barbed wire. They're clever enough to avoid poisons and traps, so farmers have virtually no way of controlling these sneaky beasts. If you see someone as a threat, do you get wild and manipulative? Bush pigs have every angle covered, and if you try to stop them, they'll teach you a solid lesson.

- **Deep down you want others to fail:** No one wants to admit to having this sentiment, but fess up if it's true. Bush pigs trample every bit of food they can't consume, so no one else can enjoy the leftovers. What do bush pigs gain by this act of sheer selfishness? Absolutely nothing. But they always do it. Now be honest here: Do you plot the failures of others? At the very least, do you *wish* for their suffering and bad fortune?

THE DINGO

You intimidate others, and you're very methodic.

- **You instill fear in others. They know you're smarter and bolder:** Driven by an insatiable hunger, dingoes go after any animal that you can imagine — sheep, calves, kangaroos, rabbits, and many others. When the Europeans

SNEAKY

came to Australia in the 18th century, they immediately
went after these smart, dangerous dogs but to very little
avail. Do you find that others are afraid of you because
you're smarter and more daring? Are you tough and
unpredictable, yet clever and calculating?

- **You're one step ahead of the competition. No one
  keeps you down:** Herdsmen have often tried to employ
  men called "doggers" to go out and catch dingoes. These
  men have had virtually no luck because of the dingo's
  unique cleverness, intelligence, and great vitality. Only
  with poison can one hope to kill a dingo, and even then the
  chances are slim. If you have overcome great adversity in
  your life, you very well may be a dingo person. Have you
  survived a disease, an accident, or a brutal enemy?

- **You're a very methodic, routine person:** Dingoes
  travel along very regular routes. They move along the coast
  during the winter, and head inland during the warm weather
  to raise their young. Is your life headed along a very distinct
  path? If you're like the dingo, you dictate the course of
  your life. You rarely allow yourself to go with the flow.

- **You're a survivor:** Legend has it that dingoes evolved
  from domesticated dogs abandoned in Australia. These
  dogs had no choice but to adapt and hunt for themselves.
  Dingo people fend for themselves, and they're born
  survivors.

THE PHASMID OR STICK INSECT

*You use sneakiness when you need to, but
you're generally fun and pleasant to work with.*

- **You don't like being sneaky, but you think it's
  sometimes necessary to get by:** Phasmids, or stick
  insects, have to worry about hungry predators every day.
  Fortunately for these fascinating insects, they can
  camouflage better than almost any other animal in the
  wilderness. Their superior camouflage accounts for their
  name, which comes from "phasma," the Latin word for
  "phantom." Phasmids look almost exactly like leaves or
  sticks, so they blend with their surroundings perfectly.

Some are as long as 15 inches to really nail down that delicate, twiggy look. Their clever disguise may be sneaky, but they only do it to avoid danger. If you have some benign tricks up your sleeve that you use to avoid problems, you may be a phasmid.

- **You're smart enough to know that you need the help of others to achieve your goals:** Phasmids and ants have a wonderful symbiotic relationship. Phasmids can't adequately protect their eggs on their own, so they enlist the help of ants. Each of the eggs has a little knob called a capitulum, which attracts ants. When the ants locate the knobbed eggs, they carry them back to the privacy of their underground nests where they eat the knob and let the egg hatch safely. The ants get some nutrition, while the phasmids get to procreate. The attachment of a knob to these eggs is a sneaky but effective way of obtaining help for the phasmids. Do you recognize that you need other people to help you? Do you use clever ways to entice others to join you?

- **But you're clever enough to get by on your own if need be:** In some phasmid species, females can reproduce without the help of males! In fact, males don't even exist in some species of these insects. Even though many phasmids can reproduce alone (through a process called "parthenogenesis"), eggs that are fertilized by males usually have a much better chance of hatching. Still, this unique potential shows that phasmids are smart enough to get help, but they're also clever enough to get by on their own if they have to. Do you find clever ways to make it on your own when you don't have anyone to help you?

- **You like to dance and have a good time:** When phasmids feel the vibration of footsteps (or even music) they let it loose and begin to dance! Well, sort of. Phasmids "dance" to simulate the swaying motions of twigs and leaves. When you're at a party, do you occasionally stop by the refreshments table? So do phasmids! When they feel a breeze, they tend to feed, which makes them feel more comfortable about moving around. The phasmid's dancing may not be fun at all, but since they move to the music, we count it as partying. Do you like to listen to music, dance, and have fun?

SNEAKY

- **You don't look like a dangerous person, but your sneakiness can be used to confront others if they ask for it:** Most phasmids are not aggressive, but if threatened, they can employ some sneaky tricks against their enemies. Some emit a chemical spray that can cause temporary blindness and lots of pain. Others release very unpleasant odors. And still others use the large spikes on their legs to swing at predators. Are you a non-aggressive person who has a latent sneaky side? If others provoke you, do you try to outsmart them with trickery?

CHAPTER 4

So You're a Dependent Animal

"Am I really a dependent person?" you might be asking. "I'm caring and daring, I'm fun and sweet. I'm outgoing and cool, I'm responsible and neat!" Well, that may be true, but you probably also need to boost your confidence and spend less time hanging on to other people.

Then again, maybe it's not so bad. Just because you're dependent doesn't mean you're not at all industrious or curious. It does mean, however, that your insecurities might overshadow some of your more redeeming qualities. As you go through the animals in this chapter, you'll see that many of them have some great traits. So don't let yourself panic too much yet. But we will say this: Spend less time judging yourself and more time exploring interesting animals!

That being said, it's time to begin our journey through the next personality test. Without further ado, we present **Chapter 4: The Dependent Animal**.

Now that you know you're a dependent animal, take this short test to find out which specific animal you resemble most.

1. Do you seek lots of attention from people?

○ YES   If you chose YES, go to question 2.
○ NO   If you chose NO, go to question 5.

2. Even though you're dependent, do you usually try to help yourself and others?

○ YES   If you chose YES, go to question 3.
○ NO   If you chose NO, go to question 4.

3. How often do people try to avoid you? Rate yourself from 1 (not often) to 3 (very often).

○ 1   If you chose 1, you are an OXPECKER.
○ 2   If you chose 2, you are a SEA SLUG.
○ 3   If you chose 3, you are a LAMPREY.

4. How often do you need to be around other people? Rate yourself from 1 (not often) to 3 (very often).

○ 1   If you chose 1, you are a BIG BROWN BAT.
○ 2   If you chose 2, you are a CHUCKWALLA.
○ 3   If you chose 3, you are a HOUSE CAT.

5. Do you communicate well with others?

○ YES   If you chose YES, go to question 6.
○ NO   If you chose NO, go to question 7.

6. How confident do you feel about your ability to contribute to the world? Rate yourself from 1 (not very) to 3 (very).

○ 1   If you chose 1, you are a PANDA.
○ 2   If you chose 2, you are a LEECH.
○ 3   If you chose 3, you are a CLEANER WRASSE.

7. Are you a playful person?

○ YES   If you chose YES, you are a KILLER WHALE.
○ NO   If you chose NO, you are a BONOBO.

THE LAMPREY

You cling to people and activities, but you take rejection well.

- **You won't leave others alone. You drive them crazy:** Lampreys are parasitic fish found in all bodies of water. Adults attach their sucker mouths onto a host fish so they can gradually eat its body and suck down its bodily fluids. At first, the hosts don't mind that much. But as time goes by, they start to get weak and sick. If you're like a lamprey, no one really enjoys your company. They'll tolerate it for a while because they have no choice, but eventually, you drive others crazy.

- **Despite your clinginess, you're a pretty quiet person:** When these parasitic fish aren't clinging to their hosts, they spend a lot of quiet time in muddy nests with other lampreys. The dark mud on the bottom of streams allows them to hide peacefully. So even if you're an overbearing nuisance, you might also redeem yourself with some personal quiet time.

- **When you don't have anyone to cling to, you'll often cling to an activity:** During spawning season, lampreys build their nests by sucking stones and dropping them in place. In other words, when these fish aren't sucking the life out of others, they're latching onto another "sucking" activity. Do you always have to latch on to someone or something?

- **People take active measures to exclude you:** Do you notice others going out of their way to keep you at a distance? If so, you have yet another similarity to the lamprey. Since lampreys kill valuable fish, many states have tried to reduce their population. If you're like a lamprey, you've probably felt that coldness from others. It's not that people think you're evil, just a little overbearing.

- **You're willing to stand up to potential rejection:** Adult lampreys attack all sorts of fish including trout, whitefish, smelt, pike, white sucker, black buffalo, brown bullhead, carp, rock bass, walleye, and paddlefish. Lamprey people look for love in all places. Most impressively, however, lampreys will latch on to armored species like sturgeons and gars. Even though these animals can be dangerous, lampreys seek them out anyway. Does an overwhelming need for belonging compel you to hang around the wrong people?

THE SEA SLUG

You're insecure and showy, but you try to help yourself.

- **You use flashiness to attract people:** Most sea slugs are bright blue or purple, which tends to scare most enemies away. If you wear flashy clothing, you might be trying to get attention from others, but like the sea slug, it ultimately keeps people at a distance. That's not to say you should be ashamed of being bold, but most blatant attempts to attract people fall terribly flat.

- **Your insecurity leaves you vulnerable to abuse:** Because of your insecurity or your high expectations of others, you often feel mistreated. The sea slug is pretty similar. It lacks a shell and therefore can have a tough time defending against predators who want to go in for the kill.

- **Still, you do your best to stand up for yourself:** Even though sea slugs have no protective shell, they can sometimes effectively use *cerata* or club-like projections of tissue found on their backs. When a sea slug battles a Portuguese man-of-war, for example, it transfers the man-of-war's stinging cells onto its own cerata and then uses them for self-defense! No one said you weren't a creative person.

- **You allow foreign forces to guide you:** Rather than choosing a clear path for yourself, you'll go where others take you. Sea slugs swallow air and then allow themselves to drift with the water. Do you find yourself always going along with the group? If your dependency threatens your individuality, you're in the right place.

- **Even though you follow others, you can be picky and spoiled:** Sea slugs are pretty fussy eaters. Each species of sea slug specializes in only one type of prey, whether it be

DEPENDENT

sponges, hydroids, or sea squirts. Similarly, are you sometimes difficult to deal with?

THE LEECH

You keep friends for a long time, but you can be weak.

- **You never get bored of the same person:** While maintaining interest in your friends is a good thing, leech-like people latch on to one person and never give him or her room to breathe. Leeches are segmented worms that attach to blood-giving hosts. Their digestive tracts have large lateral pouches that can store enough blood to feed the leech for months. That is, a leech is content for a long time when connected to just one other animal. Is your happiness contingent on any one person? If that person allows you constant contact, is it enough to make you happy?

- **You have the ability to help other people:** A Leech's salivary secretions contain hirudin, an anticoagulant that can prevent human blood clots. Some doctors have used leeches to help the wounded. Leeches also perform the appreciated service of decomposing rotting flesh. If you're like a leech, you have the ability to help others, even if most people don't really appreciate your company.

- **You'll declare virtually anyone your best friend:** Leeches are not at all particular about which animals they'll suck blood from. They'll drink the life out of humans, horses, cattle, fish, and mollusks. Do you think you could stand to be a little more discriminating in your attractions to people?

- **Your reputation exaggerates your weaknesses:** Even though leeches can suck blood from humans, they shouldn't be too much cause for concern. They're parasites that perform some good functions for the environment. All in all, their reputation is a bit harsh. Does your bad reputation also procede you? Even though you can be needy, do others give you a bad shake?

THE HOUSE CAT

You like attention and care, and you have fears.

- **You need others to help you eat and take care of yourself:** Since house cats were bred for domesticity, they're not prepared as a species to properly hunt for themselves. They rely upon their owners to help them eat, use the bathroom, and keep fully clean. Are you used to having someone wait on you hand and foot? If so, you might have found a good match.

- **You're intrigued by the lifestyles of others:** Many domestic cats never leave the house, but those that do often enjoy hunting small birds and mammals for sport. Cats rarely eat their catch, but they enjoy the thrill of the game. Conservationists complain about the unnatural hunting practices of some cats, which unnecessarily hurt certain animal populations. Just as house cats experiment with the hunting practiced by their larger relatives, cat-like people have a certain curiosity about other people and their ways of life.

- **You need lots of attention, and you turn nasty when you don't get it:** House cats require frequent petting and grooming, and when they're ignored, they become antisocial and grumpy. When people don't pay enough attention to you, do you get grouchy and unpleasant?

- **You have lots of fears, and you can be a little nervous:** While most feral cats are tough and bold, house cats tend to shy away from other animals. They feel nervous and threatened even when they see large inanimate objects. These fears stem from a lack of wilderness experience. Are you somewhat sheltered? Does your lack of experience makes you frightened and insecure?

THE CLEANER WRASSE

You're generous, respected, and trusting.

- **Even though you're needy, you're extremely giving:** The cleaner wrasse is a symbiotic fish that provides an essential service for larger fish at a small cost. It sets up "cleaning stations" in the ocean where it picks off parasites and dead tissue from other fish in order to get nutrients. Small crustaceans on the backs of large fish can also create a big nuisance, and the cleaner wrasse takes care of them all. If you're like the cleaner wrasse, you're very dependent on other people, but if they stick with you, you'll be a loyal and caring friend.

- **You're a peacemaker:** In the cleaner wrasse's presence, other fish lose their aggressiveness and get along very well. When this fish sets up cleaning stations at busy coral reefs, different species literally line up and wait to be cleaned. The cleaner wrasse creates one of the few situations in the ocean in which different fish species are not territorial. Are people at ease in your presence? Do you make people feel good about themselves?

- **Other people want to protect you:** While the cleaner wrasse performs its cleaning duties, larger fish almost never harm the wrasse. In fact, they even protect the wrasse from potential predators. This relatively small fish is, therefore, safer in the company of all of these predators than it would be swimming alone outside the cleaning stations. Do other people tend to stand up for you? Do they repay you with loyalty?

- **You're a very trusting person — sometimes even too much:** When the cleaner wrasse goes to work on another fish, it will even swim right inside the fish's mouth to clean inside. Obviously, you can see that wrasses are a trusting species. Every once in a while, however, a wrasse will become a casualty during a dental cleaning. It's rare, but it happens. Wrasse people are trusting and giving, which can make them a bit vulnerable.

THE OXPECKER

You're helpful, gossipy, and social.

- **You readily help others:** The oxpecker is a small bird that spends most of its time on the backs of rhinos and antelopes. It eats ticks and insects that would otherwise infect the large animal. Without these hosts, however, the oxpecker might not find a sufficient source of insects for food. They're very dependent, therefore, but they still earn their keep.

DID YOU HEAR THE LATEST?

- **You can be pretty irritating, but people tend to like you anyway:** Rhinos and antelope develop painful open wounds because of the oxpecker's incessant pecking, but they tolerate it anyway in exchange for the benefits. The wounds last for life, but they're better than life-threatening infection. If you're like the oxpecker, people find you irritating, but they know you're a good person.

- **You like to gossip and spread the latest news:** Oxpeckers warn their hosts of incoming danger. When they see a predator, they let out a shrill call to get away ASAP! The oxpecker's acute sight and hearing allow it to spot animals from incredible distances. Are you good at finding out important information? Do you like to spread it around to others?

- **You have a strong sense of community:** Oxpecker breeding involves not two, but five different birds at once! While only two of them actually mate, all five help choose a home spot and build the nest. When the eggs hatch, all five help with feeding and childcare. If you're truly like the oxpecker, you have a selfless devotion to your community. You understand your responsibilities to others, and you fulfill them well.

- **You like to give yourself some good "R & R":** While oxpeckers work hard for other animals, they tend to rest during the hottest part of the day. Their communal lifestyle allows for some downtime here and there. Oxpecker people are not the workaholics of the "Industrious" category. They'll take a vacation when they want one.

THE BONOBO

You're romantic, relaxed, and self-aware, but a bit devious.

- **You trust your family to the death. You rely upon them more than anyone else:** When bonobo chimpanzees get in a fight, their family members come to bail them out. They're very dependent upon one another's protection for their safety. If you're like a bonobo, you're less of a tough, loner type and more of a dependent, group type.

- **You're very intimate and physical with others:** Bonobos are famous for using sex as a means of social bonding. Males have sex with males, females with females, and adults with children. Bonobos always face each other when having sex to enhance the intimacy of the experience.

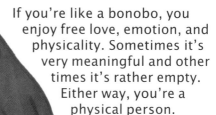

If you're like a bonobo, you enjoy free love, emotion, and physicality. Sometimes it's very meaningful and other times it's rather empty. Either way, you're a physical person.

- **Even though you need the help of others, you're generally a relaxed person:** Bonobos are much more relaxed and friendly than other animals. If you're like a bonobo, you're not very nervous or competitive. You're also not as insecure as many other people, although you'll still call your family to help you when you're in a tough bind. Bonobos live in large social groups, and they tend to get along well with one another. They depend heavily on the loyalty and work of one another, but they appreciate each other's company. Are you very social? Do you have lots of friends? If you're like a bonobo, you like to be a part of a big, secure group.

- **You're just a little bit devious:** If a bonobo sees some food, it might wait until his friends leave so that he can eat it all by himself. These animals aren't horribly sneaky or back-stabbing, but they can be a bit sly. Every once in a while, do you reveal a little deviousness?

- **You know yourself well. Even though you're needy, you're aware of it:** Bonobos are among the only animals that can recognize themselves in a mirror. They use their reflection to make sure they're fully clean, and they have a sense of their own identity. All in all, you have your insecurities and your excessive needs, but at least you understand your personality. You don't hide the fact that you're insecure, and you might be in the process of trying to reduce your dependency on others.

THE PANDA

You're emotional, communicative, and you like amenities.

- **You need lots of amenities at your constant disposal:** Pandas require about 40 pounds of bamboo every single day! And they do nothing but eat for 20 hours of every day. Why do they eat so much bamboo? Pandas used to be carnivores, but their diets evolved faster than their digestive systems. Their intestines are too short to properly digest bamboo, so they have to eat tons of it to compensate. Do you also need an excess of things to keep you happy? If you're like the panda, you seem to need (or just want) more than everyone else needs.

- **Even though you're needy, you're not dependent on other people:** Pandas are very solitary animals. Aside from mating, they live entirely alone. Since pandas can see each other's distinctive patterns from far away, they can be sure to maintain some distance. Sometimes pandas can recognize one another but only because of contact during breeding season. If you stick to yourself, you share something with the panda. Are your needs more material than social? If so, you may have a good match for yourself.

- **While you stick to yourself, you have some good communication skills:** Pandas are able to relay all sorts of relevant information simply by spraying their urine. When a panda detects the scent of another's urine, it can determine its sex, age, breeding condition and other vital information. These messages are especially important for pandas since they don't have a large accessible breeding community in a tight location. Panda people might be quiet and solitary, but they're able to say a lot in a few words. They know how to get their points across.

- **You can get very emotional — even depressed:** When a female Panda's cub dies, she can fall into a dark depression for days. She will cry incessantly and remain in one spot without eating. Do you have the tendency to get depressed when things aren't going well? Have you ever stopped taking care of yourself because of your sadness?

- **You don't like to get stuck in one place or situation:** Even though pandas move slowly and clumsily, they manage to roam across almost a mile of land every day. With the decreasing bamboo population, this movement has become increasingly important. If you get bored easily or you're afraid of inertia, you may want to consider yourself a panda.

THE BIG BROWN BAT

You're needy, prescient, and sometimes generally indifferent.

- **You don't mind letting others support you financially:** Big brown bats primarily inhabit man-made urban buildings where they hang from rafters, hide in cracks, and burrow in insulation. Some retreat to caves, where they hang in the entrance, but most prefer the luxury of an eight-story New York brownstone. People that are like big brown bats are fully capable of supporting themselves, but they prefer living off of someone else.

- **You're a give-and-take person:** Are you the type that expects a lot from others because you give a lot? If that's the case, you're like the big brown bat. They heavily rely upon farms to attract insects to eat, and in turn, they reduce a potential threat to crops. If these farms didn't exist, big brown bats would have a tougher time finding insects to consume. Unfortunately, many farmers kill these bats, confusing them with their cousin, the crop-eating fruit bat.

- **You enjoy having friends but you're just as happy without them:** Big brown bats often live with a large group, but they also often live in a solitary space. They don't seem to show a preference between having their own dens or sharing them with others. Are you relatively

DEPENDENT

indifferent about these sorts of social matters? Are you happy with or without the presence of other people as long as you're supported financially?

- **You're a good planner, and you have sharp foresight:** These bats don't eat at all during the winter. Instead, they eat a lot before the cold weather sets in and store up large fat deposits. The stored fat holds them over for the season. If you're good at preparation, you would probably do well as a big brown bat.

- **You often get what you want because you know to move quickly:** Big brown bats can fly at speeds of 40 miles per hour, enabling them to catch wasps, ants, plant hoppers, leafhoppers, June hoppers, and stinkbugs. Success often goes to the person who tries to seize it first. Are you quick to snatch opportunity for yourself?

THE CHUCKWALLA

You like to be near home, and you like to impress others.

- **You're a hometown guy or gal. You'll never stray too far:** Chuckwallas are large vegetarian lizards that escape their predators by wedging themselves in between rock crevices and then inflating themselves with air. Since they depend upon this means of survival, they can never stray too far from these havens. If you never leave your hometown, whether by choice or circumstance, then keep reading.

- **You have a strong sense of pride:** When all else fails, chuckwallas can sometimes defend themselves with their powerful bite. Against hawks, coyotes, bobcats, and foxes, however, their bite can't do too much. Still, these lizards maintain pride by fighting to the finish, even in a losing battle.

- **You try to impress the opposite sex with your riches:** Male chuckwallas attract females by staking out prime rock territory with some foliage. Those that procure the best spots get to mate the most. If you try to attract people based upon your possessions rather than your character, you're similar to the chuckwalla.

- **You pretend to be a tough one, but you're mostly putting on a show:** Chuckwallas try to scare away enemies by looking tougher than they actually are. They'll engage in bluff battles in which they'll arch their backs, bob their heads up and down, and open their mouths menacingly. In the end, these lizards are far less capable of defending themselves in a face-to-face battle than their toughness suggests. Are you a small person who compensates by acting aggressive? Are you all talk?

THE KILLER WHALE

You've suffered hardships and you follow others, but you're pretty playful.

- **You're a follower. You usually do what others do:** Killer whales live in groups or "pods." Some are part of full-time resident pods and others are only part of transient, part-time pods. Either way, when killer whales travel together, they all breathe and dive in perfect unison! Perhaps this cooperation keeps things organized and moving along, but it certainly indicates an absence of individuality. Do you follow other people?

- **Still, you have the potential to be your own person:** Even though these whales travel in groups and exhibit synchronized behavior, each has his own unique dialect of whistles, clicks, and calls for communicating with others. Despite your tendency to follow others, do you recognize that you still have the potential to be a true individual?

- **Hardships in your life have shaped your growth:** Killer whales have nicks and scars on their dorsal fins, which are testimony to their dangerous encounters. Their scars come from boats or quarrels with other animals. Scientists use these marks to identify individual killer whales. Have you had rough experiences that have greatly influenced you?

- **You depend on your family very much:** Female killer whales can live up to 70 years, so many traveling pods are matriarchal, spanning several generations. The transient, part-time pods may be less focused on the family. The killer whales in those groups have a range of 900 miles,

DEPENDENT

instilling fear in prey such as sea otters, sea lions, whales, and seals. But the many killer whales who live in resident pods are less ferocious and more dependent on the stability of their family. Are you very dependent upon your family members?

- **You enjoy a good time, and you like to have fun:** You spend lots of time around others, and you like to be silly and have fun with them. Killer whales have been known to flip 180-pound harbor seals in the air and toss them around like a tennis ball! These whales are huge and powerful, but they like to have a good time every once in a while. Since you're constantly around other people, do you find yourself goofing around and enjoying yourself pretty often?

CHAPTER 5

So You're a Curious Animal

You're probably pretty pleased right now. After all, who doesn't want to be associated with truth and discovery, brains and playfulness? You're a curious person and most likely quite interesting to be around.

Now, curiosity can manifest itself in many ways. You might be the playful, fun type; the adventurer and daredevil; the brainiac reader; the puzzle solver; or the gossip. Most curious people are pretty knowledgeable and many are very smart. We're willing to bet that you're no exception.

In fact, you've probably already scanned this book through and through. Do you devour movies, conversations, periodicals, books, and speeches? Do you like challenges and puzzles? Do you seek the truth in your work and in your daily life? Yes. Yes, you do.

But are all curious people really this smart and commendable? Well, no. Some use their hunger for knowledge towards evil ends. Others just obsess with petty facts and chit-chat. And still others like to learn but lack the I.Q. of the smarter folks. Despite these different brands, curious people all show a hunger for knowledge, and many are smart and playful.

So now it is that time. That time to harness your curiosity. Go forth and satiate your hunger for truth. Complete the next test.

Now that you know you're a curious animal, take this short test to find out which specific animal you resemble most.

1. Do you enjoy math puzzles?

○ YES   If you chose YES, go to question 2.
○ NO   If you chose NO, go to question 5.

2. Do you enjoy analyzing other people?

○ YES   If you chose YES, go to question 3.
○ NO   If you chose NO, go to question 4.

3. How patient are you? Rate yourself from 1 (not very) to 3 (very).

○ 1   If you chose 1, you are a MANTIS SHRIMP.
○ 2   If you chose 2, you are a SEA OTTER.
○ 3   If you chose 3, you are a MEERKAT.

4. Do you get yourself into trouble often?

○ YES   If you chose YES, you are a MARTEN.
○ NO   If you chose NO, you are a GIANT OCTOPUS.

5. Are you a particularly playful person?

○ YES   If you chose YES, go to question 6.
○ NO   If you chose NO, go to question 7.

6. Just how playful are you? Rate yourself from 1 (a little playful) to 3 (very playful).

○ 1   If you chose 1, you are a DOLPHIN.
○ 2   If you chose 2, you are an OSTRICH.
○ 3   If you chose 3, you are a COATIMUNDI.

7. Are you a cocky person?

○ YES   If you chose YES, you are a DEGU.
○ NO   If you chose NO, you are a MANATEE.

THE MEERKAT

You're smart, patient, and unique.

- **You're very eloquent and well-read:** Meerkats belong to the Mongoose family, and they live primarily in South Africa. They have extraordinary vocabularies, which enable them to communicate well with each other. Meerkats are highly intelligent and are capable of expressing complex ideas. Are you a well-spoken, true intellectual?

- **You pace yourself well and have a good sense of your abilities:** Meerkats seek out soft sand when digging for food because it's easy to penetrate. They can then devote extra energy to digging through compact sand to build sturdy homes. People who resemble meerkats accomplish a lot because they know how to manage their time. Do you believe in doing things the right way the first time?

- **You have a certain mental toughness that gets you through hard times:** Because of metabolic adaptations, meerkats are able to get by on much less food and water than other animals. Their metabolic rates are 40 percent slower than similar animals in different parts of the world. Only the toughest of humans are able to get by with little food and water. If you want to be a Meerkat, you had better be sharp and mentally tough.

- **You're not a morning person:** Believe it or not, meerkats lose five percent of their body weight overnight! Even though they may not eat a ton, the impoverished meerkats need to find food as soon as they get up to regain all of that lost energy. Do you wake up feeling awful in the morning? Does your entire body seem to ache? Do you need a hearty breakfast and some major stretching to get in gear for the day?

- **You're a unique thinker:** Each meerkat has a unique set of markings on its back, symbolic of its self-assuredness and personal abilities. While meerkats work well with others, each one is smart enough to look out for itself. Are you an independent thinker who can also work well in groups?

- **You love to observe and scrutinize:** Meerkats have exceptional eyesight. In fact, they're able to see clearly even while looking directly into the sun. In the desert, they remove sand from their eyes by blinking rapidly. Unfortunately, meerkats don't have great depth perception, and they see objects better at a distance than from close-up. Still, they love to observe, just like any other curious intellectual. Do you enjoy looking around and examining things?

- **You're not impulsive. You develop well-thought-out strategies:** When meerkats sense danger, they band together in a group and devise a plan of defense. They're very adept at responding to different situations. This sense of strategy and cooperation shows a synthesis of logic and creativity. Do you often come up with smart, new ideas?

THE GIANT OCTOPUS

You don't look very smart, but you're clever, curious, and selfless.

- **People might assume you're just a big jock, but you're actually a smart, curious person:** The giant octopus can weigh as much as 100 pounds, and a few have even reached up to 400 pounds! As the largest octopus species, this ocean monster might seem like an enormous, dumb blob, but it's anything but that. The giant octopus is not particularly dangerous (they almost never try to hurt scuba divers), and is very intelligent and curious. If people think you look like a big football jock, but you're actually more of an academic type, you're not unlike the giant octopus.

- **You're a good, selfless person:** When a female giant octopus lays her eggs by a rocky den, she guards them for about seven straight months, never even breaking for food. Shortly after the eggs hatch, the mother will die from exhaustion and malnutrition. These sea creatures are clearly the epitome of parental love. People who are like giant octopuses readily make big sacrifices for others. Are you a good, generous person?

CURIOUS

- **You like to explore, but you appreciate quiet time in the comfort of your home:** Even though giant octopuses love to feel around and explore their surroundings, they rely heavily upon their dens for mating and for protection. They also catch food and enjoy it in the comfort and safety of their homes. If you're constantly running around town and you get bored in your house, you're not a giant octopus type.

- **You assume the best in people. You give others the benefit of the doubt:** When a scuba diver comes into contact with a giant octopus, the octopus will wrap its feelers all around the diver and explore his or her body. The octopus isn't interested in scaring the diver, it just wants a chance to learn about its visitor. The octopus, although capable of strangling and stinging its enemies, assumes only the best about human visitors. They're not afraid of us, and they're not interested in bothering us. If you assume people are inherently good, you're just like the giant octopus.

- **Despite your good nature, you know how to handle those that get in your way:** Giant octopuses have a number of sea predators to worry about, including seals, sharks, and other large octopuses. They defend themselves by squeezing their soft bodies into tight crevices, changing colors to camouflage themselves, squirting ink, stinging with their tentacles, and biting with their strong mouths. All in all, giant octopuses aren't ocean beasts, but they're smart enough to defend themselves in a variety of ways. Are you fairly gentle with a latent capacity to be cunning and tough?

- **You like to learn and you're very good at it:** The giant octopus has the largest brain of any mollusk. They have good memories and can learn complicated tasks. Do you like to memorize and learn new things?

THE MANATEE

You're goofy and likable, but slightly naive.

- **You like to live on the edge. Sometimes you don't account for possible danger:** These curious "sea cows" love to check out everything that comes into their path.

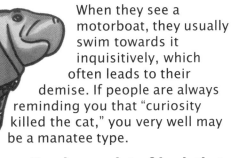

When they see a motorboat, they usually swim towards it inquisitively, which often leads to their demise. If people are always reminding you that "curiosity killed the cat," you very well may be a manatee type.

- **You have a lot of junk that you don't need:** Curious people often have a ton of stuff that they never throw out. The manatee, too, has something that it surely doesn't need. On each of its two flippers, it has three to four nails, which are entirely vestigial. That is, the manatee evolved from a land animal that most likely used the nails for defense or for cutting, but these nails now serve no purpose for this underwater creature.

- **You're the big, goofy, lovable type:** Manatees can weigh up to 2,000 pounds, but they're just harmless vegetarians. They never cause fights, and they spend most of their time relaxing, drifting, and eating. This one's straightforward. If you're a big, gentle giant, you probably know it.

- **You're a good traveler:** Manatees have remarkable stamina when moving through the water. Every winter, they migrate south and swim up to 45 miles in a single day! They find food along the way, so they don't have to prepare before departing. Of course, some manatees are better travelers than others. All in all, though, these slow-moving animals have great stamina, which tremendously helps their traveling.

- **You don't forget easily. It's very possible you've held on to bad memories:** Unfortunately, almost every manatee has scarring on its back from motorboats. Scars are so common that scientists use them to identify manatees in the wild. Some of the scars are superficial, and new skin covers the wound, but others last for the manatee's entire life. If you're like a manatee, you may have emotional scars or bad memories that are hard to escape.

CURIOUS

THE SEA OTTER

You're smart and playful, and you analyze others well.

- **You like to wear very nice clothing:** Sea otters don't have insulating blubber as other marine mammals do, so they rely upon their beautiful fur coat to stay warm. Their fur is finer and denser than that of any other animal in the world! In fact, sea otters have about 650,000 hairs per square inch of their bodies. Do you like to be fashionable like the sea otter?

- **You love to play! You enjoy having fun and goofing around:** If you're playful and you like silliness, you've found your match. Sea otters love to play around with each other, teasing and roughhousing all the time. They're bold, curious animals that enjoy toys and swimming fast.

- **You tend to be a bit compulsive and possibly even a little vain:** Sea otters spend about 48 percent of daylight hours grooming their fur. They do so with their strong claws, and they roll around in the water afterwards to smooth themselves. If you're not terribly compulsive or vain, you can still be a sea otter if you're very playful. But if you share these traits too, there's no question you've found the right animal.

- **You're resourceful, smart, and accomplished:** In order to crack open mollusk shells, sea otters smash them against a rock sitting on their chest. The methodic clicking that can be heard as a sea otter attempts to get at its food shows this animal's determination and ingenuity. Are you smart and effective?

- **People try to use you for their own gain:** Sea otters used to be hunted by the thousands; now they're caught by the hundreds. Heavy hunting for their furs has greatly depleted the sea otter population, earning them a "threatened" status on the endangered species list. Various sea birds show us a more benign use of the sea otter's offerings. They fly around above these marine mammals, waiting to snatch any dropped food. These birds aren't really stealing so much as cleaning up the mess. So, people try to take advantage of sea otter types.

THE OSTRICH

You like control and expediency, but you know how to enjoy yourself.

- **You like to do things quickly:** Ostriches are the fastest living animals on two legs, reaching speeds of up to 44 miles per hour! Weighing about 300 pounds, the ostrich is certainly not your typical bird. Do you like to move quickly in everything you do?

- **You fight for your own well-being. You can be a little selfish here and there:** Ostriches lay their eggs in a communal nest. There can be as many as 40 eggs in a nest at one time. Since only 20 or so can be incubated, the dominant hen will decide which stay and which go. Of course, she makes sure that all of hers get to stay in the nest. Since parental protection is very natural, we say that ostriches are a little selfish but not horrible. If you look out for yourself, sometimes maybe a little too much, you're similar to the ostrich.

- **You're a big believer in gender equality:** Ostrich hens incubate their eggs during the day, and the cocks do it at night. Since the hen has more prenatal responsibility than the cock, the cock will take care of the chicks once they're born. Males will fight with one another, and the weaker of the two will often run away, abandoning his chicks. The victor, in that case, raises the chicks as his own. All in all, males play their part and females play theirs. Do you also value equal opportunity and responsibility for men and women?

- **You like to play or relax in the water:** Do you enjoy water parks? Swimming in the ocean? Well, ostriches absolutely love to kick back in the water. They love to bathe, wade, and just splash around. Just as we look out for our safety in water parks, ostriches have to avoid ravenous alligators and other predators when they're hanging out in the water. In general, though, these huge birds love to play in the water without a care in the world.

- **You like to feel in control. You know what's going on in your life, and you analyze yourself often:** Ostriches sit on the grass so they're less detectable by

CURIOUS

predators, and they use their long necks as a periscope to survey their surroundings. They're smart and know how to keep safe, and they're also curious about activity in their environment. The sitting position, therefore, satisfies the ostrich's need for protection and its bug for curiosity.

THE MANTIS SHRIMP

You're fickle, smart, and too curious about other people.

- **You like to spy on other people (or at least eavesdrop):** These beautifully-colored shrimp hide under rocks and coral, and they peer their heads out just enough to check out the scene. They love to observe scuba divers, in addition to any foreign object that comes their way. Their eyes sit at the end of long, periscopic stalks, which helps them spy. If you love gossip or spectacle, and you're sometimes willing to eavesdrop or spy to get it, you're just like the mantis shrimp.

- **You're very defensive. You want people to know not to mess around with you:** Mantis shrimp use their pointy claws to thrash anything that poses a remote threat. They may be small, but they're incredibly tough for their size. Some spear their enemies, and some smash them with their hammer-like elbows. Their claws have cut off divers' fingers, and their smashes, which can have the power of a small-caliber bullet, have broken through aquarium walls! These little marine creatures get the message out loud and clear: "We're vicious, so get away." Are you a loose cannon? Do you have a very distinct tough side?

- **You lose interest in boyfriends/girlfriends quickly:** When a male mantis shrimp is in heat, it enters a female's burrow to mate. Once the female loses interest in the male, she aggressively sends him out of her burrow. No explanations offered. Gone. The male has no choice but to move on, even though he usually wishes to stick around. If you get bored with girlfriends or boyfriends very easily, you're similar to the heartless mantis shrimp.

- **Not only are you super-smart, everyone else knows it:** Mantis shrimp are a source of awe for any observer. They can strike in $1/125^{th}$ of a second, they can spot prey anywhere, they can camouflage themselves, and they're not afraid of anything. Perhaps even more impressive, however, is the genius of these curious, tough animals. Their intelligence allows them to elaborately stalk their enemies and maximize their highly-evolved senses. Now, you need to be honest and ask yourself: Are you a genius? Does *everyone else* think you're a genius?

THE DEGU

You're outgoing, cocky, and begrudging.

- **You love meeting new people:** Degus are curious, social rodents that love to play with one another. They'll even interact with other, unthreatening species. They're generally very gentle, and they get excited at the prospect of observing others. Are you curious about different cultures and making new friends?

- **People know you as a chatterbox:** These interesting rodents are extremely vocal, making all sorts of whistling, chatty sounds. They're very communicative animals, and when they can't chat often, they're easily prone to depression. Do you love conversation and general chit-chat? Do you get sad when you're alone too long?

- **You're not the "forgive-and-forget" type:** Do you hold long grudges? If a person or another animal mistreats a degu, it will never forget it. Degus remember individual enemies and won't hesitate to seek revenge later. Degu types are friendly and playful unless you're unkind to them.

- **You have an off-beat sense of style:** Unlike almost any other animal, degus have bright orange teeth! In fact, white teeth indicate that a degu is about to die. Do you wear funky colors and march to your own beat?

CURIOUS

- **You tend to brag now and then**: Degus let out a "wheep" sound to attract mates, and they let out a similar post-mating cry to brag about their conquests! They're not terribly proud animals, but they like others to know about their good fortune. If you're like the degu, you enjoy recognition from others, and you're not shy about telling them about your exploits.

THE COATIMUNDI

You're interested in gender issues, you're rebellious, and you appreciate subtlety.

- **You appreciate that there's more to life than the obvious:** Coatimundis are curious, raccoon-like mammals found in Central America. They eat all sorts of fruits and small animals, but they're smart enough to search in unique places for buried treasures. They examine small crevices for tasty rodents, and they'll even break apart rotting logs to find some good insects. They use their manual dexterity and their intelligence to find food in special places. Do you take things at face value or do you look beyond the obvious to find answers?

- **You think that men have had their opportunity for power, and now it's time for women to take control:** Coatimundis travel in groups of about twenty, and acceptance is always determined by the female. Outside of mating season, the females won't even allow males into the group, and during mating season, the males remain at the mercy of the females. Do you appreciate this gender dynamic?

- **You enjoy old-fashioned playgrounds and other physical activity:** Coatimundis love to climb, explore, swing on ropes, and fool around with toys. They're mischievous and love to get attention from one another.

They hang out in trees and like to pick through trash for food (and out of curiosity). People who are like coatimundis have a child-like, playful energy.

- **You're prone to a little rebellion (at least in your younger years):** At about six months of age, coatimundis can become somewhat unruly and rebellious, defying their mothers and trying to cause trouble. People who own coatimundis as pets have to deal with these youthful outbursts of bad behavior. Do you have a bad temper? Do you look to mess around with people now and then?

THE DOLPHIN

You think all the time, you like most people, and you care for yourself well.

- **You think a lot about every little thing you do:** Since dolphins are mammals, they breathe air just like we do. Unlike humans, however, their breathing isn't involuntary; they have to think to keep breathing. When they feel the need for more air, dolphins surface, open their blowholes and get a fresh breath. If you're like the dolphin, you think about all of the detailed, mundane aspects of your life.

- **You believe in constant communication. You're very social:** Dolphins communicate with one another using vocalizations, which are sounds created by the blowhole. These sounds allow them to convey complex ideas with one another. In addition, dolphins use echolocation, or sonar, to navigate through murky water. They release clicking sounds, and use echoes to avoid swimming into objects. Do you talk about complicated ideas with other people? Do you ask people for directions to make sure you're on the right path?

- **Rather than having a few close friends, you prefer to have tons of friends around you as often as**

CURIOUS

possible: Dolphins travel in schools of up to 1,000! By traveling in a big group, the dolphins have a better chance of avoiding sharks and killer whales, and they're able to enjoy each other's company. They like to play with one another and explore the ocean together. Do you like having lots and lots of friends around all the time?

- **You like to eat fresh, healthy foods. You care about your body:** Dolphins have a developed sense of taste that allows them to make sure a fish is fresh. They won't eat any food that has started to spoil. They care about their bodies, trying to build up a layer of insulating blubber. Are you a health food nut? Do you work out at the gym all the time? Are you often aware of how your eating affects your appearance?

THE MARTEN

You're scatterbrained, hyper, and more curious than almost everyone.

- **You're hyper, nervous, and super gossipy:** Martens are house-cat-size members of the weasel family. And while you might associate weasels with sneakiness, martens are primarily *fidgety* and *excitable*. These agile animals let out a low, raspy sound whenever they're nervous or curious, which is almost all the time. Martens have an overall nervous demeanor, and they're always dashing through the forest. If you talk too fast or you get nervous and excited easily, you're almost definitely a marten.

- **You take everything just a bit too far. You're a person of extremes:** Martens love to eat blueberries, crowberries, and cranberries. In fact, they eat so many, that their lips and their poop actually turn BLUE! These little eccentric mammals clearly take things to the extreme. Do you tend to take things too far?

- **You're the type who would use a metal detector on a beach:** Do you love to find little treasures here and there? Are you a bit of a scavenger? Martens love to run up and down beaches searching for all sorts of food in their typical hyper fashion.

- **You're scatterbrained and often disorganized:** Martens don't look for food in a very methodic manner. Instead, they erratically cover about five miles every day. If they smell food or hear any sort of sound, they immediately scurry over to check it out. If you're like the marten, you act on your whims, and you don't do well with organization.

- **Your need for gossip and your curiosity get you in trouble:** Since martens check out every single sound and every last smell, they're easy to catch. One researcher, in fact, used some jam to catch the same marten 77 times! They're not unintelligent animals, but they just can't control their curiosity. Do you share this problem?

CURIOUS

CHAPTER 6

So You're a Simple Animal

We'll keep the words nice and short on this one. You wouldn't have it any other way, right? Chances are you're not the brightest star in the intellectual sky. You don't like complexity, and things tend to confuse you pretty easily. Overall, you like simple pleasures, so it's not too tough to satisfy you.

Does that make you a dumb person? No. People in the simple category just like to keep things straightforward and easy. You might not have the brainpower to engage tough questions, or you might just prefer avoiding anything that requires you to flex your intellectual muscles. It remains to be determined.

Is it possible that you're actually very smart, but you've learned that happiness stems from the simpler things in life? Sure. If you're in this category, though, the chances are good that you're not too well-equipped to grapple with major cerebral challenges. Then again, you might have some deep-down smarts, but maybe you're just a bit too gullible and confused.

Whatever the case, there's no reason to get down about it. We're certain that you have lots of wonderful traits to contribute to the world. But since you landed yourself right into Chapter 6, you might as well get to filling out this chapter's personality test. Here we go...

SIMPLE

Now that you know you're a simple animal, take this short test to find out which specific animal you resemble most.

1. Are you a forgetful person?

○ YES   If you chose YES, go to question 2.
○ NO   If you chose NO, go to question 5.

2. Are you pretty good at using logic to solve problems?

○ YES   If you chose YES, go to question 3.
○ NO   If you chose NO, go to question 4.

3. Are you mischievous?

○ YES   If you chose YES, you are a MOTH.
○ NO   If you chose NO, you are a GOLDFISH.

4. Are you a very content person?

○ YES   If you chose YES, you are a COW.
○ NO   If you chose NO, you are a SHEEP.

5. Are you often gullible or oblivious to your surroundings?

○ YES   If you chose YES, go to question 6.
○ NO   If you chose NO, go to question 7.

6. Just how gullible or oblivious are you? Rate yourself from one (pretty gullible/oblivious) to 3 (very gullible/oblivious).

○ 1   If you chose 1, you are a BASS.
○ 2   If you chose 2, you are a MOOSE.
○ 3   If you chose 3, you are a WILD TURKEY.

7. Are you a very passive person?

○ YES   If you chose YES, you are an ARMADILLO.
○ NO   If you chose NO, you are an AMOEBA.

THE WILD TURKEY

You're insecure and gullible.

- **You prefer casual connections to longer, meaningful relationships:** Turkeys are polygamous birds that try to mate as much as possible. The males flaunt their colorful plumage to attract females. After mating, though, the males move on to new opportunities elsewhere. Turkeys are the playboys of wild birds. Do you dislike long-term commitment in your relationships? Do you need your dating freedom?

I FINISHED THE CROSSWORD TODAY.

- **You compensate for your deficiencies by bragging about unimportant accomplishments:** These big birds are well known for a few special traits. They have excellent hearing, despite not having visible ears. They also have long legs that let them move around quickly. Obviously these traits are useful but probably not worth bragging about. If you're like the wild turkey, everyone knows about the mundane successes in your life.

- **You have a tough time discerning fiction from reality:** Believe it or not, turkeys are afraid of...TREES! Well, sort of. Some people believe that turkeys can mistake certain trees for dangerous predators. Better to be safe than sorry, yes, but these turkeys have no excuse for this kind of mix-up. If you believe too much of what you read, you're a bit like the wild turkey.

- **You're oblivious to the fashions around you:** While male wild turkeys can look somewhat attractive with their colorful feathers, females commit the faux pas of sporting facial hair! Although not all female turkeys commit this fashion sin, many do have long tufts of facial hair. Turkey people just don't have a sense of the coolest fashions.

- **You're pitifully gullible:** Wild turkeys are suckers for the contrived "bird calls" of hunters. When people belt out the cackle, the purr, the kee-kee-run, or the gobble, the turkeys come running. Do you fall for tricks all the time? If you were somewhat savvier, would you avoid trouble more often?

THE SHEEP

You're forgetful and not very thoughtful.

- **You can't seem to learn not to bite the hand that feeds you:** Most people know not to mistreat their providers. If you just can't learn this lesson, you've got something in common with the sheep. These woolly animals insist on head-butting people who feed them, not out of self-defense, but simply out of habit. If you leave a pail of food out for a sheep, it'll head-butt the pail for no reason. Not a very intelligent maneuver.

- **You have no idea how to defend yourself:** Shyness is not an excuse for not knowing any self-defense. All remotely intelligent people have thought about survival tactics in the face of danger. Sheep, however, can't seem to figure out how to take care of themselves. In 1999, one little poodle killed 20 sheep in England! Are you as incapable as a sheep? Do you find trouble in seemingly easy situations?

- **You don't have good self-control. You're also not too good at problem-solving:** If a sheep falls on its back, it can't get back up on its own! This inability doesn't speak well for these mammals. If you can't control yourself, you're just like a sheep.

- **You forget everything all the time:** When sheep get ticks or fleas, they spend so much time scratching and rubbing against fences that they actually *forget to eat!* If a sheep loses a lot of weight, it may very well have some sort of itchy parasite on its wool. Do you forget everything that you're supposed to remember? Do you forget things that seem *impossible* to forget?

SIMPLE

- **You never question authority:** Sheep graze as if they're all tied together. In fact, if a dangerous animal approaches a flock, they can't even manage to run away as individuals. They end up walking all over one another and creating "shear" chaos! If you're like a sheep, you tend to follow others instead of asserting your own individuality.

THE MOTH

You're good at meeting members of the opposite sex and you're mischievous, but you don't command much respect.

- **You don't do well with details:** Even though moths are supposed to travel towards moonlight to keep their direction, they can't tell the difference between the moon and outdoor porch lights. Ever notice the swarm of moths around lightbulbs outside? It's all a matter of a missed detail: A porch light is not the same as the moon. Do you miss details that can be crucial at times?

- **People take advantage of you often:** When most moths are in the caterpillar stage, they're very vulnerable to a whole host of predatory beetles and spiders. Every time a caterpillar molts, it gets larger, but never large enough to avoid attacks. Moreover, caterpillars remain completely still for days during molting, so they're especially open to attack. If you're like a moth, people pick on you pretty often.

- **You may not be the smartest person, but you know how to find a date:** Like some other animals, moths release pheromones to attract mating partners. Their sense of smell allows them to detect one another from miles and miles away! If you know the hot spots to find good-looking men or women (and you're pretty good at meeting them), you're similar to the moth.

- **You're mischievous, but you rarely get away with anything:** Some moth species produce larvae in human clothing so that the offspring can feed on the fabric. Sometimes, however, the little grubs will inch their way out of the clothing and onto walls or ceilings where they're usually seized and flushed down the toilet. Do you not think about danger very often? Do you often get yourself into trouble because you don't think things through?

- **You're greedy, and you can be disrespectful:** In addition to clothing destruction, some moth larvae destroy mass quantities of green foliage and lots of fruit. If you're selfish and you don't adequately respect other people's things, you share something with the moth.

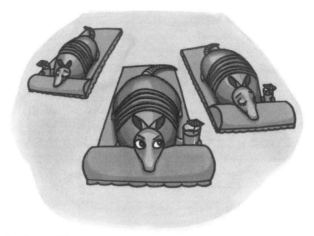

THE ARMADILLO

You're passive, possessive, and indulgent.

- **You're a drifter:** When armadillos cross bodies of water, they swallow lots of air, which inflates their intestines. Then they just float around almost effortlessly. Are you very relaxed? Do you float through situations?

- **You can be pretty desperate to get your fill of simple pleasures:** Even though armadillos eat small snakes and lizards, they'll actually resort to digging up and eating dead bodies! If the body is too much of a mess to eat, they will rip it open and devour the maggots found inside! They suck them right out with their long noses. For an animal that uses its tough armor to kill prey, the armadillo resorts to some pretty desperate tactics. If you'll do anything to get some extra pleasure, you're a bit like the armadillo.

- **You hate it when other people touch your things:** Like many other animals, armadillos mark their territory by spraying their urine. But these armored mammals are so serious about protecting their property that they'll spray even until they're dehydrated! If you wash away the armadillo's urine, it'll continue spraying until it loses so much body fluid that it dies. So even though you're a drifter, you're serious about protecting your stuff.

- **You're not good at dealing with people:** Armadillos have armor for protection, but in the face of danger, they'll often run away or quickly burrow into the ground. When a coyote sees the protruding armor of a buried armadillo, it simply pierces through the motionless animal and enjoys an easy victory. Clearly not the best defensive tactic. Are you pretty bad at handling other people? Are you in need of problem-solving advice?

- **You feel like you're a dime-a-dozen:** All of an armadillo's offspring are genetically identical! That means that when you see an armadillo somewhere, you can bet there are others that are EXACTLY the same somewhere else. Armadillos are the only mammals that always do this. If you feel like just another brick in the wall, like just another checker on the checkerboard, you've got something in common with the armadillo.

THE MOOSE

You get yourself into rough situations, and you often feel slighted.

- **You obliviously walk into danger:** If you don't think before you act, you might have something in common with the moose. Although this is not terribly common, some moose dive right into lakes in very deep, dangerous rock quarries! These moose would surely die without professional rescue help.

- **You have little sense of impossibility:** Many overzealous moose try to mate with cows that have not yet come into estrus. Obviously, their advances are always rejected. Even when the cows kick the males in the head to get the point across they'll still try making attempts at other moose that are too young! If you can't seem to grasp a sense of what's possible and what is not, you're similar to the moose.

- **You only know how to settle disputes through fighting:** Like many other animals, moose bulls fight one another during mating season. But the fights are more ritualistic than anything else. They rarely establish any dominance or accomplish any other practical function. Do you just fight for the sake of fighting? Do you not know how to effectively solve problems?

- **You feel that you weren't born with certain abilities that could help you get what you want:** Moose love to eat fresh grass in the early summer, but they have trouble reaching it because their legs are too long and their necks are too short. They have no choice but to kneel awkwardly, and even then, they can't get all that they want. Moose people just don't have certain important natural abilities. Do you feel that you were born inferior to others in some ways?

SIMPLE

THE GOLDFISH

You value routine and health, but forget things often.

- **You have a terrible memory:** Goldfish have a memory span of only three seconds! Not too good. Since they have such poor memories, they can forget that they just ate and eat again and again if food is available. In fact, goldfish owners must make sure not to overfeed their fish because they'll eat to their death. You could say that these fish are so simple, it's dangerous. In the wild, however, goldfish probably don't have to worry about the danger of too much available food. Even so, they're simple fish with horrible memories. Do you have trouble remembering things that you shouldn't forget?

- **You live a slow-paced, routine life, which helps you stay healthy:** Goldfish are peaceable animals, and they can live for a very long time. In the wild, they can live for about 15 years, but in captivity, some end up living up to 50 years. They don't require difficult care, and their needs are simple. If you're a quiet, healthy person, you're not unlike the goldfish.

- **You spend a lot of time on your appearance and beauty:** Of the 20 different kinds of goldfish, many are fancy and stunning. Chinese and Japanese breeders helped create many of the interesting types that we see today. When goldfish are placed in flowing bodies of water like lakes or rivers, they lose their beautiful luster and become dull and plain-colored. So, great efforts are taken to make sure that the goldfish we see in aquariums or small ponds are unique and pretty. Do you focus on appearance to compensate for other deficiencies?

- **You're not an easy sleeper:** Goldfish don't have any eyelids, so they need shade to go to sleep. Do you need the perfect bed, the perfect temperature, and perfect darkness to go to sleep? Although being a picky sleeper is not central to being a goldfish person, it's a small part of the package.

THE COW

You're not logical, but you're frisky and content.

- **You don't employ logic very well:** Cows have been known to walk right into sharp barbed-wire and thorny cactuses. They can't seem to anticipate the pain that they bring upon themselves. Even trial and error doesn't fully nip the problem in the bud. If you often have trouble putting two and two together or linking cause and effect, you're very much like the cow.

- **You're not good with names and faces:** Most other mammals are better than cows at recognizing individual humans. Cows probably can't recognize their owners well even though they interact with them everyday.

- **You're almost always content. You never search for something more:** Cows stand up and sit down only fourteen times per day. That means that once they're sitting, they stay there for a long time. If you're always pleased with your lot and you never hope for something better or aspire to something higher, you have a cow-like quality.

- **You can get a little frisky when you're feeling in shape:** Lactating cows produce over 60 pounds of milk every single day. It's important, therefore, that farmers milk them to alleviate the building pressure. After a thorough milking, the cows feel much better, and they'll even behave a little friskily. Do you tend to get a little more spirited when your body feels good?

THE AMOEBA

You're not opinionated, and you close yourself off from most people.

SIMPLE

- **You don't have fully-formed opinions about issues:** Amoebas are microscopic single-celled organisms that live in water, soil, or living bodies. Their bodies are entirely shapeless and change appearance as they move. Do your opinions and beliefs constantly change like the amoeba's body? Do you lack your own set of views?

- **But you are discerning about who you allow into your life:** Amoebas have a thin, elastic membrane that holds the cell together. Water and only certain gases can pass through this semi-permeable border. That way, the amoeba can be sure to take in only useful substances. If you're like an amoeba, you may not think about complex

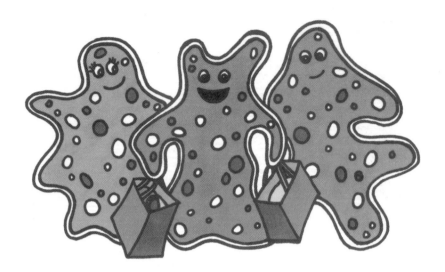

political issues or big moral quandaries, but you do think about who you value as a friend.

- **You sacrifice for your family:** Even though you're a simple person, you're willing to give things up for your family. Amoebas reproduce through a process called fission in which they split in half, forming two amoebas. In other words, these single-celled organisms literally give up their bodies to give way to new life. Are you also sacrificing for the members of your family?

- **You can get on people's nerves now and again:** One type of amoeba can cause serious illness in humans. If someone ingests this type of amoeba, he or she will come down with a terribly unpleasant case of amebic dysentery. Not a pleasant experience by any means. Amoeba-like people have the tendency to bother people every once in a while. Do you fall into this category?

- **You like shopping and making purchases:** Amoeba people are not especially greedy, but they do like to have a lot of possessions. When an amoeba sees a piece of food that it wants to ingest, it actually creates arms (or pseudopods) to grab its prize! Amoebas move their jelly-like cellular fluid into arms that engulf the food into the cell. If you're like an amoeba, you like owning things.

THE BASS

You believe too easily, and you like variety.

- **You're gullible and easily tricked:** Bass are pretty easy to catch compared to most other freshwater fish. If you throw a lure or some bait in the water, chances are you'll have no problem tricking these fish into biting. If you catch a bass and throw him back, it's not impossible that he'll fall for the same trick again later! Perhaps these poor fish aren't to blame; after all, humans go to great efforts to perfect the sport of duping these animals. Still, they get tricked time and time again. If people are always scamming you, you're like a bass. Do you believe too much? Are you not sufficiently skeptical?

- **You may not be very bright, but at least you've got muscles:** Even though bass are not the most difficult catch for fishermen, they're extremely tough fighters for their size. They fight hard to the finish, even though they're usually overpowered by man in the end. Are you all muscles, little brains?

- **Your size fluctuates a lot:** Individual bass do not actually change size that dramatically, but their size range across their population is astonishing. Spotted bass, for example, can weigh as little as one pound at full size, while a jewfish (a sea bass) can weigh up to 700 pounds! Most spotted bass are about seven inches long, but jewfish can measure up to over eight feet! Does your size change from time to time based on your habits and lifestyle?

SIMPLE

- **You enjoy different climates and locations:** Do you like the sun as well as the snow? Do you like urban settings as well as more rural spots? Sea bass can survive in both fresh water *and* salt water. Because of the damming of inland waters where they breed, however, some now only live in fresh water. If you don't have strong feelings one way or the other about your climate, you have a similarity to the bass.

WHICH TYPE OF ANIMAL IS THAT CELEBRITY?

A fun sampling

By now you've probably figured out what animal you're most like. In this final part of the book, we've picked out some big celebrities and matched them with different animals from the six chapters. Just wait until George W. Bush finds out he's a sea otter!

Madonna: The Coatimundi

We easily placed Madonna into the Curious Animals category. She seems to go through frequent phases, exploring all sorts of groups, activities, and lifestyles. Coatimundis are rebellious, and we know that Madonna has shocked the world with her rebelliousness time and again. She's a powerful woman, which fits with the coatimundi value of female control. Finally, coatimundi types appreciate subtlety, which fits with Madonna's thoughtfulness and her mystique.

Woody Allen: The Marten

Although Woody Allen could have fallen into a couple of categories, we ultimately linked him with the marten of the Curious Animals. Martens are hyper and nervous, and they always take things to extremes. This seems a perfect match for the characters Woody Allen plays in his movies. Even Woody Allen's love life is full of surprises and extremes, just like the marten. These weasel-like animals get themselves into trouble because of their eccentricity, and we know that Woody Allen has been the subject of criticism because of many of his personal choices.

Drew Barrymore: The Killer Whale

There's no question about it: Drew Barrymore is 100 percent killer whale. Just as killer whales are known to be followers, Drew Barrymore followed in the footsteps of the many actors in her family. Killer whales are shaped by the hardships they endured growing up, and we know that Drew Barrymore struggled with drugs and alcohol at a very young age. Just as killer whales love to have to fun, Drew Barrymore has a playful spirit and loves to go out partying. She's just about as killer whale as they come.

Bill Gates: The Meerkat

Meerkats are smart, patient, and unique, and Microsoft founder Bill Gates likewise has these qualities. His curiosity and ambition compelled him to leave college to develop personal computers. Without perseverance, patience, and confidence, he could never have achieved his goals. Meerkats like to scrutinize and strategize. These are traits that Bill Gates, as the biggest CEO in the world, certainly has. Meerkats are also known to be very tough, and Bill Gates has been ruthless — some might say too ruthless — in pursuing his business interests.

Mother Theresa: The Cleaner Wrasse

Even though cleaner wrasses are in the Dependent Animals chapter, they're not terribly dependent on individual people. Rather, they need the opportunity to be helping others in order to be happy. For Mother Theresa, a world peacemaker and humanitarian, the cleaner wrasse is a perfect match. Like this fish, she was trusting and giving, and she worked hard to promote peace. People still praise her work and her contributions to society, just as other fish show their love and appreciation for the cleaner wrasse by protecting it.

Mike Tyson: The Moose

The moose is the perfect example of a simple fighter, just like former heavyweight boxing champion Mike Tyson. Moose solve problems with fighting, just like boxers. Moose walk into danger all the time, and they have little sense of the impossible. Mike Tyson has a long history of walking into legal trouble because of careless decisions. Additionally, we speculated that moose might be bitter that they're born without certain attributes that could help them succeed. Similarly, Mike Tyson comes from a disadvantaged background. He's the perfect moose.

Martin Luther King, Jr.: The Leaf-Cutting Ant

Martin Luther King, Jr. stood for ideals, and he fought inequality and discrimination with all his might. A sincere, intimate person, he embodied hard work for a noble cause. Leaf-cutting ants are intimate, hard-working creatures. We linked them with detesting discrimination and promoting social consciousness. They're stable and confident and make tremendous daily progress toward their goals. Martin Luther King, Jr. exemplified these qualities.

Napoleon Bonaparte: The Short-Tailed Shrew

As an iron-fisted, small man, French dictator Napoleon Bonaparte is about as short-tail shrew as they come. These rodents command much more power and ferocity than their size would ever suggest. They like to be left alone to work hard, and they don't like to play with others. Napoleon was a harsh, businesslike ruler despite his meager stature. He challenged countries bigger than his own, just as the short-tailed shrew fights larger enemies.

Tiger Woods: The Beaver

Beavers accomplish a lot in a little time, just like golf sensation Tiger Woods. He worked very hard from a young age, turned pro early, and has succeeded ever since. We said that beavers have a skill for landscape architecture, which seems fitting for someone who spends all day on the golf course. We linked beavers to people who upgrade their lifestyles when they get more money, and Tiger Woods, with all his new wealth, is certainly able to live more luxuriously now. For a successful, serious, hard worker like Tiger Woods, the beaver is an ideal match.

Conclusion

Congratulations! By now you should know exactly what animal you are. We hope you had fun journeying through the animal kingdom, and we hope you've learned a little bit about yourself, too. From now on you'll look at zoos and pet stores in a whole new light. Thanks for reading this book, and have a wonderful day.

Jeremy Bronson grew up in Scarsdale, NY. He graduated from Harvard College in June 2002, where he majored in Government. He was an editor of the *Harvard Lampoon* and the *Harvard Political Review*. But more important, he is clearly a meerkat.

Liz Phang grew up in the Washington, DC area. She graduated from Harvard College in June 2002, where she majored in English and was an illustrator for the *Harvard Lampoon*. She is not ashamed to say that she is a dependent animal — an oxpecker, to be specific. She lives in Austin, Texas.